THE

RULES OF MANAGEMENT

A Definitive Code for
Managerial Success

EXPANDED EDITION

RICHARD TEMPLAR

Vice President, Publisher: Tim Moore
Associate Publisher and Director of Marketing: Amy Neidlinger
Aquisitions Editor: Megan Colvin
Senior Marketing Manager: Julie Phifer
Assistant Marketing Manager: Megan Colvin
Cover Designer: Alan Clements
Managing Editor: Kristy Hart
Senior Project Editor: Jovana San Nicolas-Shirley
Proofreader: Apostrophe Editing Services
Senior Compositor: Gloria Schurick
Manufacturing Buyer: Dan Uhrig

© 2011 by Pearson Education, Inc.

Publishing as FT Press
Upper Saddle River, New Jersey 07458

Authorized adaptation from the original UK edition, entitled *The Rules of Management*, Second Edition, by Richard Templar, published by Pearson Education Limited, © Pearson Education 2011.

This U.S. adaptation is published by Pearson Education Inc, © 2011 by arrangement with Pearson Education Ltd, United Kingdom.

FT Press offers excellent discounts on this book when ordered in quantity for bulk purchases or special sales. For more information, please contact U.S. Corporate and Government Sales, 1-800-382-3419, corpsales@pearsontechgroup.com. For sales outside the U.S., please contact International Sales at international@pearson.com.

Printed in the United States of America

First Printing May 2011

ISBN-10: 0-13-273310-2
ISBN-13: 978-0-13-273310-6

Pearson Education LTD.
Pearson Education Australia PTY, Limited.
Pearson Education Singapore, Pte. Ltd.
Pearson Education North Asia, Ltd.
Pearson Education Canada, Ltd.
Pearson Educación de Mexico, S.A. de C.V.
Pearson Education—Japan
Pearson Education Malaysia, Pte. Ltd.

Library of Congress Cataloging-in-Publication Data

Templar, Richard, 1950-2006.
    The rules of management : a definitive code for managerial success / Richard Templar. — Expanded ed.
        p. cm.
    Rev. ed. of: The rules of management : a definitive code for managerial success. 2005.
    ISBN 978-0-13-273310-6 (pbk. : alk. paper)
    1. Management. 2. Executives. 3. Executive ability. I. Title.
HD31.T45 2011b
658—dc22
                                        2011011469

Contents

Part II Managing Yourself **79**

Introduction

Strange thing, management. It's something few of us set out in life to do, yet most of us find ourselves doing at some point.

Careers adviser: What would you like to do when you leave school?

16-year-old: I want to be a manager.

Did this happen to you? No, me neither. But here you are anyway.

As a manager you are expected to be a lot of things. A tower of strength, a leader and innovator, a magician (conjuring up pay raises, resources and extra staff at the drop of a hat), a kindly uncle/aunt, a shoulder to cry on, a dynamic motivator, a stern but fair judge, a diplomat, a politician, a financial wizard (no, this is quite different from being a magician), a protector, a savior and a saint.

You are responsible for a whole gang of people that you probably didn't pick, may not like, and might have nothing in common with and who perhaps won't like you much. You have to coax out of them a decent day's work. You are also responsible for their physical, emotional, and mental safety and care. You have to make sure they don't hurt themselves—or each other. You have to ensure they can carry out their jobs according to whatever rules your industry warrants. You have to know your rights, their rights, the company's rights, and the government's rights.

And on top of all this, you're expected to do your job as well.

Oh yes, and you have to remain cool and calm—you can't shout, throw things, or have favorites. This management business is a tall order....

You are responsible for looking after and getting the best out of a team. This team may behave at times like small children—and you can't smack them* (or possibly even fire them). At other times they will behave like petulant teenagers—sleeping in late, not showing up, refusing to do any real work if they do show up, quitting early—that sort of thing.

Like you, I've managed teams (in my case, up to 100 people at a time). People whose names I was expected to know and all their little foibles—ah, Heather can't work late on a Tuesday because her daughter has to be picked up from her play group. Trevor is color blind, so we can't use him at the trade show.

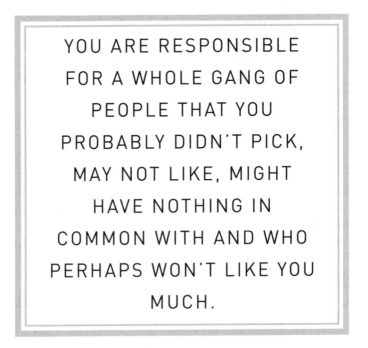

YOU ARE RESPONSIBLE FOR A WHOLE GANG OF PEOPLE THAT YOU PROBABLY DIDN'T PICK, MAY NOT LIKE, MIGHT HAVE NOTHING IN COMMON WITH AND WHO PERHAPS WON'T LIKE YOU MUCH.

* Yes, yes, I know you can't smack children either. I was just making a point. Please don't email me.

Mandy sulks if left to answer the phones at lunchtime and loses customers. Chris is great in a team but can't motivate herself to do anything solo. Ray drinks and shouldn't be allowed to drive anywhere.

As a manager, you are also expected to be a buffer zone between higher management and your staff. Nonsense may come down from on high but you have to a) sell it to your team, b) not groan loudly or laugh, and c) get your team to work with it even if it is nonsense.

You also have to justify the "no pay raises this year" mentality even if it has just completely demotivated your team. You will have to keep secret any knowledge you have of takeovers, mergers, acquisitions, secret deals, senior management buy-outs and the like, despite the fact that rumors are flying and you are being constantly asked questions by your team.

You are responsible not only for people but also for budgets, discipline, communications, efficiency, legal matters, union matters, health and safety matters, personnel matters, pensions, sick pay, maternity leave, paternity leave, holidays, time off, time sheets, tight deadlines and leaving presents, industry

> AS A MANAGER, YOU ARE ALSO EXPECTED TO BE A BUFFER ZONE BETWEEN HIGHER MANAGEMENT AND YOUR STAFF.

standards, fire drills, first aid, fresh air, heating, plumbing, parking spaces, lighting, stationery, resources, and tea and coffee. And that's not to mention the small matter of customers.

And you will have to fight with other departments, other teams, clients, senior bosses, senior management, the board, shareholders and the accounts department. (Unless of course you are the manager of the accounts department.)

You are also expected to set standards. This means you are going to have to be an on-time, up-front, smartly dressed, hardworking, industrious, late-staying, early-rising, detached, responsible, caring, knowledgeable, above-reproach juggler. Tall order.

You also need to accept that as a manager you may be ridiculed—think *The Office*—and possibly even judged by your staff, shareholders and the public to be ineffective and even superfluous to the carrying out of the actual job in hand.*

And all you wanted to do was your job.... Luckily there are a few hints and tips that will have you sailing through it looking cool, gaining points, and coming up smelling of roses. These are *The Rules of Management*—the unwritten, unspoken, unacknowledged Rules. Keep them to yourself if you want to stay one step ahead of the game.

---

* If this all makes you feel a bit bleak about being a manager—don't be. Managers are the stuff that runs the world. We get to lead, to inspire, to motivate, to guide, to shape the future. We get to make a difference to the business and to people's lives. We get to make a real and positive contribution to the state of the world. We get not only to be part of the solution but also to provide the solution. We are the sheriff and the marshal and the ranger all rolled into one. We are the engine and the captain. It's a great role and we should relish it—it's just not always an easy role....

Management is an art and a science. There are textbooks of thousands of pages devoted to how to do it. There are countless training courses. (You've probably been on a few.) However, what no textbook contains and no training course includes are the various "unwritten" rules that make you a good, effective and decent manager—the *Rules of Management*. Whether you are responsible for only one or two people or thousands—it doesn't matter. The Rules are the same.

You won't find anything here you probably didn't already know. Or if you didn't know it, then you will read it and say, "But that's really obvious." Yes, it is all really obvious, if you think hard enough about it. But in the fast-paced, frantic, just-about- coping kind of life we lead, you may not have thought about it lately. And what isn't so obvious is whether you do it.

It's all very well saying "But I know that already." Yes, as a smart person you probably do, but ask yourself honestly for each rule: Do you put it into practice, carry it out, work with it as standard? Are you sure?

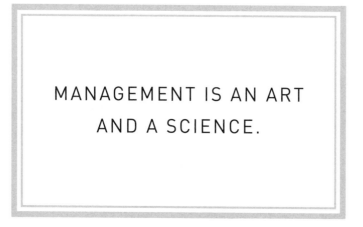

MANAGEMENT IS AN ART
AND A SCIENCE.

I've arranged these Rules for you into two sections:

- Managing your team
- Managing yourself

I think that should be fairly simple. The Rules aren't arranged in any particular order of importance—the first ones aren't more important than later ones or vice versa. Read them all and then start to put them into practice, adopting the ones that seem easiest to you first. A lot of them will flow together so that you can begin to carry them out simultaneously, unconsciously. Soon we'll have you looking cool and relaxed, confident, and assertive, in charge, in control, on top of things, and managing well. Not bad considering it wasn't too long ago you were shoulder to the wheel, nose to the grindstone, ear to the ground and back to the wall. Well done you.

SOON WE'LL HAVE YOU LOOKING COOL AND RELAXED, CONFIDENT, AND ASSERTIVE, IN CHARGE, IN CONTROL, ON TOP OF THINGS, AND MANAGING WELL.

Before we begin, it might be worth taking a moment or two to determine what exactly we all mean by "management." And that isn't as easy as it sounds. For my money we are all managers—parents, the self-employed, the entrepreneur, the employed, even the ones who inherited wealth. We all have to "manage." It might only be ourselves, but we still have to cope, to make the best use of the resources available, motivate, plan, process, facilitate, monitor, measure success, set standards, budget, execute, and work. It's just that some of us have to do all that with bigger teams. But the fundamental stuff doesn't change.

The Harvard Business School defines a manager as someone who "gets results through other people." The great management consultant Peter Drucker says a manager is someone who has the responsibility to plan, execute, and monitor; whereas the Australian Institute of Management definition of a manager is a person who "plans, leads, organizes, delegates, controls, evaluates, and budgets in order to achieve an outcome." I can go along with that.

It can get very wordy and complex:

> A Manager is an employee who forms part of the organization's management team and is accountable for exercising delegated authority over human, financial, and material management to accomplish the objectives of the organization. Managers are responsible for managing human resources, communicating, practicing and promoting the corporate values, ethics and culture of the organization, and for leading and managing change within the organization. (The Leadership Network, California)

Fine, whatever. We are all managers in whatever form or shape we think, and we all have to get on with the job of managing. Anything that makes our life simpler is a bonus. Here are the simple Rules of Management. They aren't devious or

PART I

MANAGING YOUR TEAM

We all have to work with people. These may be loosely known as a team or a department or a squad or a crew—even a posse. It doesn't matter. The mistake a lot of managers make is to think they are managing people. They think that people are their tools, their stock-in-trade. Make the people successful and you have the successful manager—or so the theory goes.

But unfortunately this is a myth, and we need to see that the real role of the manager is to manage processes rather than people. People can manage themselves if you let them. What you need to be concentrating on is the real job of management—the strategy. The team is merely a means to fulfilling that end. If all your people could be replaced by machines—and how many of us haven't prayed that this might happen?—we would still need a strategy, still need to manage the process.

Of course we, as managers, have to work with real flesh-and-blood people, and we have to know what motivates them, how they think and feel, why they come to work, why they give their best (or their worst), what they are afraid of, what they hope and dream for. We shall have to encourage them, coach them, give them the resources to do their job and manage themselves, oversee their processes, and set their strategy for them. We will worry about them, look out for them, be on their side, and support them. But we won't manage them. We will let them manage themselves, and we shall concentrate on our real role as a manager.

RULE 1

Get Them Emotionally Involved

You manage people. People who are paid to do a job. But if it is "just a job" to them, you'll never get their best. If they come to work looking to clock in and clock out and do as little as they can get away with in between, then you're doomed to failure, my friend. On the other hand, if they come to work looking to enjoy themselves, looking to be stretched, challenged, inspired, and get involved, then you have a big chance to get the best out of them. Trouble is, the jump from drudge to super team is entirely up to you. It is you that has to inspire them, lead them, motivate them, challenge them, and get them emotionally involved.

That's OK. You like a challenge, don't you? The good news is that getting a team emotionally involved is easy. All you have to do is make them care about what they are doing. And that's easy, too. You have to get them to see the relevance of what they are doing, how it makes an impact on people's lives, how they provide for the needs of other human beings, and how they can reach out and touch people by what they do at work. Get them convinced—because it is true of course—that what they do makes a difference, that it contributes to society in some way rather than just lines the owner's or shareholders" pockets, or ensures that the chief executive gets a big fat pay check.

And yes, I know it's easier to show how they contribute if you manage nurses rather than an advertising sales team, but if you think about it, then you can find value in any role and instill pride in those who do whatever job it is. Prove it? OK. Well, those who sell advertising space are helping other companies, some of which may be very small, reach their markets.

They are alerting potential customers to things they may have wanted for a long time and may actually need. They are keeping the newspaper or magazine afloat as it relies on ad sales income, and that magazine or newspaper delivers information and gives pleasure to the people who buy it. (Otherwise they wouldn't, would they?)

Get them to care because that's an easy thing to do. Look, this is a given. Everyone deep down wants to be valued and to be useful. The cynics will say this is nonsense, but it is true, deep down true. All you have to do is reach down far enough, and you will find care, feeling, concern, responsibility, and involvement. Bring all that stuff up, and they'll follow you forever and not even realize why.

Oh, just make sure that you've convinced yourself first before you try this out on your team. Do you believe that what you do makes a positive difference? If you're not sure, reach down, deep down, and find a way to care....

> GET THEM CONVINCED—
> BECAUSE IT IS TRUE OF
> COURSE—THAT WHAT THEY
> DO MAKES A DIFFERENCE.

Know What a Team Is and How It Works

So what is a team and how does it operate? If we are going to be successful managers we have to know the answers to these questions.

A team isn't a collection of people. It is an organization with its own dynamics, qualities, and conventions. Without knowing these things, you will flounder. Knowing them, you can work your team to achieve greatness.

In every team there are a variety of people all pushing and shoving in different directions and with unequal force. Some shove louder, if you know what I mean. Others are happy to push from the back. Others don't appear to be doing anything, but you'll need them for ideas.

If you haven't looked at team dynamics before, I urge you to read Meredith Belbin's Management Teams: Why they succeed or fail.* (If you have, go right to the next Rule.) This is designed for managers concerned with achieving results by getting the best from their key people. I'll paraphrase what he says, but I do urge you to practice what he preaches.

Belbin says that there are nine team roles—and we all carry out one or more functions of these team roles. Yes, it is fun to identify our own, but it is much more useful to identify your team's and then work with that information.

The nine team roles are the Plant (that's the ideas person), the Resource Investigator, the Coordinator, the Shaper, the Monitor Evaluator, the Team Worker, the Implementer,

---

* R. Meredith Belbin, *Management Teams: Why They Succeed or Fail*, Butterworth-Heinemann, 3rd edition, 2010.

the Completer, and the Specialist. If you want to know more, you'll have to read the book.

Now you know who you might have on your team. So what exactly is a team, and how are you going to make yours more effective? Again, read Belbin and also come to understand a team is a group where all the members focus on a collective target. A team doesn't pull together well when each individual member focuses on their own target—be that just getting to the end of the day, their own personal progress, how to appease the boss (that's you, by the way), use work as a social club, and so on.

You'll know you have a team when you hear "we" and "us" more often than "I" and "me."

You'll know you have a team when difficult decisions become easy—because someone says, "It's OK, we're all in this together."

You'll know you have a team when the team tells you it is a team.

> A TEAM DOESN'T PULL TOGETHER WELL WHEN EACH INDIVIDUAL MEMBER FOCUSES ON THEIR OWN TARGET.

RULE 3

Set Realistic Targets—No, Really Realistic

When I was doing the research for this book, someone said that setting realistic targets was unrealistic and that all targets should be "stretching" ones because that would impress the board. Now, can you see the problem here? Yep, we're not talking here about motivating a team, getting a job done, and creating an atmosphere of success and creativity. No, we're talking about impressing the board. Now on paper that might be a smart thing to do if your board is made up of monkeys, but I bet it isn't. I bet it's made up of pretty shrewd folks who would see through a maneuver like that in a nanosecond.

When I say realistic, I don't say lower or easy-to-achieve targets. I say realistic. That might mean taxing. It might mean a struggle. It might mean your team has to redouble its efforts, work harder, longer, and brighter. But Rule 3 says realistic and that means achievable, within your grasp. And yes, you might have to stretch a bit.

Realistic means you know what your team is capable of and what is expected of it by your bosses. Somehow you will have to marry the two to keep both sides happy. You can't pressure your team out of existence, nor can you let your bosses think you're slacking.

If your bosses insist on setting targets that aren't realistic, you must feed that back to them. Don't argue or procrastinate; feed it back to them. Ask how they think the targets could be achievable. Say they are unrealistic. Be very well prepared; make your case that the targets are unrealistic, and ask again how they think they could be achieved. Suggest a realistic target of your own, well supported by facts and figures. Keep feeding the problem back to your bosses and asking for clarification. Sooner or later they must set a more realistic target or order you to achieve the impossible. Either way, you are absolved of the problem. If they set realistic targets, then all you need to do is meet them. (You know you can do this.) If they order you to fulfil unrealistic ones, you are also in the clear; when you fail to achieve the unachievable, you can explain that at the time you did register your protest and bring your case back to them.

KEEP FEEDING THE
PROBLEM BACK TO YOUR
BOSSES.

RULE 4

Hold Effective Meetings...

We've all been to them—the meetings that drag on, people who ramble, agendas written on the back of an envelope or in the spur of the moment, any-other-business surprises, lack of information, and insufficient notice.

As a manager you will have to hold meetings. Make them effective. Decide in advance what the objective of the meeting is and make sure you meet that objective.

Basically, meetings have only four purposes:

- To create and fuse a team
- To impart information
- To brainstorm ideas (and make decisions)
- To collect information (and make decisions)

Some meetings might well take in one or more of these, but you should still be aware of that and add it into your objective. If your meeting is to impart information, then do it and get the hell out. If it's a discussion about that information you want, then that's a different type of meeting and as such should have different objectives.

Be aware that some meetings are there to help your team meet each other, bond, socialize together, find out about each other, and see you in your true role as team leader.

If you want your meetings to be effective, then remain firmly in control—no wishy-washy democracies here. You are the manager and you are in charge—end of story. To be effective you shouldn't allow anyone to reminisce, ramble, jabber on, or refuse to shut up or relax. Keep 'em moving fast and get them out of the door as soon as you can.

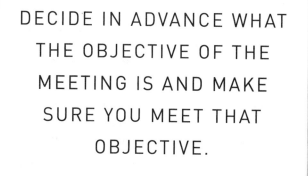

DECIDE IN ADVANCE WHAT
THE OBJECTIVE OF THE
MEETING IS AND MAKE
SURE YOU MEET THAT
OBJECTIVE.

...No, Really Effective

Right, now you're sure this meeting is necessary, and what it's for, let's keep it as brief and effective as possible.

Hold all meetings at the end of the day rather than at the beginning. Everyone's anxious to go home, and it keeps meetings shorter; at the beginning of the day, everyone has hours to digress and chat. Unless of course it is a bonding meeting; you can cheerfully hold them at the beginning of business.

See how many meetings you could hold by email, phone, or one-to-one. (Cut out everyone who isn't absolutely essential.)

Start all meetings on time. Never wait for anyone. Never go back over stuff for latecomers. If they've missed something vital, they can get it from others after the meeting, and it'll teach 'em to be on time next time. Useful tip—never schedule meetings to begin exactly on the hour, always say 3:10 p.m. rather than 3 o'clock. You'll find people will always be more punctual if you set an "odd" time. Try 3:35 p.m. if you want to be really wacky.

Schedule the meeting far enough in advance—but not too far—so that no one can say they had something else to do. Confirm the day before with everyone to make sure they have remembered and can make it.

You decide who keeps the minutes—and make sure he does, and to your liking. You don't have to be bossy or aggressive about this, just firm, friendly, and utterly in control.

Make sure every point on the agenda ends up with an action plan—no action plan means it was just a chat. Or make a decision of course.

You don't do "any other business"—ever. If it's important it should be on the agenda. If it isn't, then it shouldn't be there at all. "Any other business" is invariably someone trying to get something over on someone else. Don't allow it—ever.

If meetings are getting too big—more than six people—start to subdivide them into committees, and get your committees to report back.

And most important of all—engrave this one on your heart—all meetings must have a definite purpose. At the end of the meeting you must be able to say whether you met that purpose. Oh yes, and hold all meetings on uncomfortable chairs (or standing, à la *West Wing*)—that speeds things up considerably.

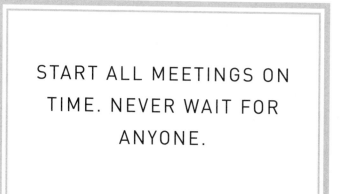

START ALL MEETINGS ON
TIME. NEVER WAIT FOR
ANYONE.

Make Meetings Fun

I guess that when you were working your way up to your illustrious position of today you had to sit through many interminable meetings, all boring, all stupifyingly dull. Well, the pattern has to be broken somewhere, and I'm relying on you to break it. The old way of doing meetings has to stop, and you're the person to do the stopping.

So let's make 'em fun. Now, before we go on, I remember a tip I read somewhere. Basically you were supposed to give out five coins to each meeting member, and when they wanted to speak, they had to spend a penny. After they had used up their coins, they were done and couldn't say anything more. It was supposed to make people really cautious about speaking and reluctant to spend all their coins on trivia. Fun? Maybe. But it would also get you quite a reputation as a prankster and an ineffectual meeting leader. As would other suggestions such as

- Formal dress
- Food and/or drink (unless it's lunchtime, in which case that's functional not fun; or if you take your team out to a restaurant or down the sports bar, and then it's not a meeting, it's a bonding session—or a thank you of course: see Rule 20)
- Games, quizzes, or contests of any sort
- Having small surprises such as chocolates taped under the chairs
- A talking stick (don't ask—a New Age Californian thing)
- Blindfolds
- Letting the most junior member chair the meeting

All of these head toward farce, ruin, and idiocy. Don't go there.

So how can you shake things up without looking like Michael Scott? Well, for a start, fun doesn't have to mean silly or stupid.

Fun means not being stuffy, allowing people to be themselves and to bring their own contribution. Fun means allowing people to share things that have made them laugh without being frowned on. Fun is about letting people tell stories or anecdotes that lighten the mood. (Just know when to say, "Right, back to business.") Fun means being flexible enough to allow other suggestions as to where and how you all meet. Perhaps your organization has a great boardroom—could you meet there? Or outside if the weather is good.

The confident manager—that's you—can be flexible because you are relaxed and cool and confident. The stuffy manager is frightened, feeling insecure, and seeking a rigid approach to prop up a lack of self-confidence.

> THE OLD WAY OF DOING
> MEETINGS HAS TO STOP
> AND YOU'RE THE VERY
> PERSON TO DO THE
> STOPPING.

RULE 7

Make Your Team Better Than You

A really good manager, yep that's you again, knows that when their team takes wing and soars, they too will soar. Getting your team to soar takes courage, grit, determination, and an overwhelming passion.

You have to make members of your team better than you, which means trusting them, getting them the best resources, training them to take over from you, trusting them not to stab you in the back when it's time to take over from you, and being confident enough in your own abilities not to be jealous of them when they do take off. Tall order.

It takes quite some manager to carry this one out. You have to be pretty relaxed and secure in your own position. Encouraging your team to bring it on takes guts, quite frankly.

Let's take a look at your team. Who've you got there? Which ones will one day fill your shoes? What can you share with them to urge them on?

Shoe-fillers are the ones you want to cultivate and grow. They are the bright ones, the keen ones, the eager beavers. I once had a young assistant who was so sharp he scared me. But when I did move on up, he filled my shoes. And he came with me over several moves, always one step behind. Now the crazy thing was he was better than me in lots of ways but he never overtook me. It could have been out of respect but I doubt it—the industry I worked in was a little cut-throat to say the least. No, it was habit.

After you've built a good team, it gets in the habit of having you as the manager, and then it feels comfortable with that and doesn't mutiny or overtake you. Teams do that only when they feel resentful or mistrusted. So bring 'em on and train 'em up and make 'em better.

AFTER YOU'VE BUILT A
GOOD TEAM, IT GETS IN
THE HABIT OF HAVING YOU
AS THE MANAGER.

RULE 8

Know Your Own Importance

You are the most important person on your team, and you'd better know it. No, not because you're a better person or more experienced or more valuable or anything to get big-headed about. You're the most important person because everyone else will take their lead from you. You set the bar.

If you play dirty, backstab, worry that your team members are better than you, spy on them, try to stop them outshining you, or are unethical, disrespectful, or anything else of the sort, then you're not going to excel as a manager, and your team members will be so busy checking over their shoulders that they won't perform, and your department won't shine.

Maybe you don't get involved in all that nasty stuff? Good, pleased to hear it. But it won't help much either if you whine, complain about directors or customers, take a negative view, resist change, talk about how much you're looking forward to Friday afternoon, always take the easy option, or avoid hard work—your team will copy all those things instead.

Listen, if you don't set the standard, raise the tone, be the person you want your team to be, then you won't be a truly great manager. Your team is like a flock of birds or sheep or, well, anything that comes in a flock.* Where one goes, they all go. And you're the one they all follow. If you shine, everyone shines. If you fail, everyone fails. Because of you. Scary, huh?

---

* Except maybe wallpaper.

But it's OK. Because you can be that brilliant manager they need to lead them. And when you are, they'll be a brilliant team full of brilliant people. Not only will you succeed personally, but you'll also bring success to everyone around you. You'll approach every task with enthusiasm backed up by solid analysis and common-sense strategies. You'll treat people around you fairly, and encourage others, and deliver better than you promised, and create a positive atmosphere, and so will everyone around you. Because of you.

IF YOU DON'T SET THE STANDARD, RAISE THE TONE, BE THE PERSON YOU WANT YOUR TEAM TO BE, THEN YOU WON'T BE A TRULY GREAT MANAGER.

RULE 9

Set Your Boundaries

You have to, right from day one, be totally on top of the discipline issue. Remember earlier we talked about how looking after your team can be a bit like being a parent? Well, as a parent you pretty well have to set boundaries and practice zero tolerance to survive. Give 'em an inch and they'll take a mile. If you are seen to be soft, they'll take advantage. The good thing with clear boundaries and zero tolerance is you have a finite line—a yardstick by which you can judge everything. All you have to do is ask, "Is this a breach of the rules?" If it is, stop it. If you do allow it, where do you stop?

Say one of your clear boundaries is timekeeping. (It might be dress or customer care or whatever, but just say it's timekeeping.) If one minute late is fine, what about two? If two is fine, what about three? And so on until people are wandering in at whatever time they feel like. But if you don't allow it, then that's the end of the story. You don't have to think about that particular issue any more. Whereas if you do allow infringements, small breaches, you are forever having to consider, "Is this a step too far?" "Can I get control back?" "How far am I prepared to go?"

This doesn't mean you need to have hundreds of rules and be ridiculously inflexible. It means that you need to decide on your few key boundaries that are important to you and to the team and the business. Make them clear. And make them firm.

Remember you are dealing with a team—I will stress this again and again throughout this book—and not an individual. You might feel that for each person an exception can be made, but you aren't dealing with individuals—you are dealing with a team. If you are seen to be soft on one individual, then you must be soft on all. If you allow one to wander in late, then all must be allowed to wander in late. If one person can get away with breaking the rules, then all must be allowed.

The good manager is firm on inappropriate behavior because this sends out a clear message to all the team—the message that you are a good, firm, in-control sort of manager who sets more store by what the team can achieve collectively than by being thought of as an easy-going, laid-back, nice person. Yes, individually some of the team may rate you as pretty cool if you let them get away with murder, but the team will collectively trash you.

> THE GOOD THING WITH
> ZERO TOLERANCE IS YOU
> HAVE A FINITE LINE—A
> YARDSTICK BY WHICH YOU
> CAN JUDGE EVERYTHING.

RULE 10

Be Ready to Prune

OK, so say you've got an orchestra and you get them to play. You listen. Something is wrong somewhere. Yep, that flute player is out of tune, off key, and playing from a different music sheet. Now you have three choices:

- Put up with it
- Change it
- End it

Let's have a little look at these three because, as in all things—from relationships, to life, to work, to being a parent—these three choices are the same every time.

So, you're going to put up with it. This makes your entire orchestra sound flat, out of tune, and ill-fitted to do its job properly—that of supplying sweet music to the masses. Your listening public (your objective) will not listen and will accuse you, the orchestra leader, of being a jerk*—and they would be right.

OK, so you're going to try to change it. Flute player X gets some retraining. He gets sent on a remedial flute course—residential of course. He returns with the right music sheet but has decided to switch to the bassoon because he was feeling creatively hemmed in by the flute. Problem sorted. Well done for tackling it.

---

* They don't of course use this word, but I'm not allowed to use the word they really would use.

However, what if his report says he is tone deaf and should never have been in the orchestra in the first place and should have taken up a career sounding the fire alarm somewhere? What you can't do is then embark on another course of action where you give him the triangle to play, but he messes that up too and by now the rest of the orchestra has lost confidence in you and is beginning to mutiny.

Time for the third course. You make him no longer needed. It is swift and kind. He can then go on to become a champion alarm ringer somewhere, somewhere else that is, and your orchestra recognizes you as decisive, knowing what you want, objective (you put the needs of the many before the bad playing of one) and utterly in charge. Have an extra brownie point.

Always be ready to prune dead wood, straggly growth, lousy flute players (and any other team players who don't cut the mustard).

> THEIR REPORT SAYS HE IS TONE DEAF AND SHOULD NEVER HAVE BEEN IN THE ORCHESTRA IN THE FIRST PLACE.

Offload as Much as You Can—or Dare

The good manager, and that is you from now on, knows that she manages events, processes, situations, strategies but never people. Look, let's imagine you have a big garden and decide to employ a gardener. Do you manage the gardener? No. He manages himself quite nicely, thank you. Your job is to manage the garden. You'll decide what to plant and when and where. The gardener, like a spade or a wheelbarrow, becomes a tool in that garden and a tool you can use to manage your garden effectively. But you don't manage the gardener. He manages himself. You tell him what you want done and he gets on with it. You delegate and he digs, and delves, and plants, and prunes, and tends, and weeds. The plants actually manage themselves as well; neither you nor the gardener actually grows anything—you both manage. The gardener is your useful assistant, your tool to getting stuff done.

Now it makes sense to give the gardener as much to do with the decision-making process as possible to free you up for long-term strategy, seeing the big picture, seasonal planning and perusing seed catalogues while sitting in the shade sipping a cold beverage.

There is no point standing over the gardener while he mows lawns, weeds beds, prunes trees, and the like. It is better to give him the job to do and then let him get on with it. After he finishes you can check his work and make sure it is up to par. And then you probably won't need to do that again—don't keep checking.

And that basically is the secret of good management. Give 'em a job to do and let them get on with it. Check once or twice to make sure they've done it the way you want it done, and then next time just let them get on with it. Increasingly give them more and more to do, and stand back more and more from the people processes and concentrate instead on the planning processes. Build your team and then trust them to get on with it. Sometimes this will backfire and people will act up, goof off, do things badly—and hey, that'll be entirely your fault because you are the manager and it's your team. No, that's serious; it is entirely up to you. Read on and we'll find ways to make sure it doesn't happen—well, not too often anyway.

BUILD YOUR TEAM AND THEN TRUST THEM TO GET ON WITH IT.

RULE 12

Let Them Make Mistakes

There is an old Chinese saying that goes something like this: "Tell me and I'll remember for an hour; show me and I'll remember for a day; but let me do it and I'll remember forever." Fair enough. And if you are going to let people do it, then they are going to do it badly at first. They are going to make mistakes. And you are going to let them.

If you are a parent, you know the agonizing thing you go through with a 2-year-old who insists they can pour her own drink—and then proceeds to spill most of it on the table. You stand by with a cloth behind your back because you know that:

- She is going to spill it.
- It is you who is going to have to mop it up.
- The spilling process is important; you have to let her do it; and she will progress to not spilling but only after she gets the spilling out of the way first.

As a parent you do that wonderful hovering thing, ready to grab the juice if it is going to spill too much, or grab the cup if it is tipping over, or even grab the child if she is going to fall off the chair due to such intense concentration.

I'm not saying members of your team are like small children—well, I am actually but don't tell them—but it is imperative you learn to let them do the spilling if they are to progress. Make sure you have your cloth behind your back ready to mop up after them.

And after each spilling you don't tell them off. Instead you offer praise—"Well done, brilliant job, incredible progress." Try not to let them see the cloth or the mopping up.

TELL ME AND I'LL REMEMBER FOR AN HOUR; SHOW ME AND I'LL REMEMBER FOR A DAY; BUT LET ME DO IT AND I'LL REMEMBER FOREVER.

Accept Their Limitations

As we saw earlier, effectively fusing a team together means you need several different parts—or team members. Now some of us are good at certain things and others not so. If we were all the same, we wouldn't be able to work as a team—we would all be leaders or all followers, and you need a combination, not either/or.

So if some members of your team aren't leaders—or followers—you have to accept that. If some are good at figure work and others not, you have to accept that. If some are good at working unsupervised and others not, you have to accept that.

And to accept these things, you have to know your staff pretty well. You have to know their strengths and weaknesses, good points and bad. If you don't—and I'm sure this doesn't apply to you—you will be forever trying to shove round pegs into square holes and vice versa.

You have to accept that not everyone is going to be as bright, as determined, as ambitious, as clever, or as motivated as you are—praise indeed from me, but see the next rule. Some of your team are quite possibly going to be brain dead from the feet up, and you might need to practice Rule 10 before Rule 13 if there simply is no hope. But don't act in haste. You might not need a team of geniuses. (In fact if you hire people far too smart for a job, they will just leave, fast.)

Suppose your team contains machine operators or admin assistants. Now you don't need these good people to have Einstein brains nor to be really on the ball when it comes to brainstorming. But you do need them to sit in a butt-numbing position for hours at a time concentrating on a bit of work that would drive you or me batty. Just don't expect them to take creative wing and soar away with new ideas, new innovations, or new technologies. You have to accept their limitations—and love them for them because these limitations are their parameters by which you can get the very best out of them—their best of course. And while you're at it, have a quick check of your own limitations. What's that? You haven't got any? Come on.

> IF WE WERE ALL THE SAME, WE WOULDN'T BE ABLE TO WORK AS A TEAM—WE WOULD ALL BE LEADERS OR ALL FOLLOWERS.

RULE 14

Encourage People

If you don't let people know you're pleased with them, they'll wilt. People come to work for a whole bunch of reasons—most, nothing to do with the money despite what they'll tell you—and right there at the top of their unwritten, unspoken, undeclared list will be "Praise from the boss." That's you by the way, the boss.

They might call it "recognition" or "acknowledgment" or "feeling I've done well"—but how do they know? They know because you tell them.

Now you can praise them retroactively, so to speak—wait until they've done good and then tell them they've done good—or you can encourage them in advance—active praise. Tell them they're going to do good before they've done it. Why? Because the chances of them doing good are that much greater if you have praised them in advance. They won't want to let you down, or themselves.

Being a manager is a minimalist's dream. You want to build a great team, and you want to do it with the smallest output of resources. Praise is free. It is instantly replaceable, doesn't wear out, is invariably 100 percent effective, is incredibly simple to do, and takes no time at all.

So why don't more managers do it? Because it takes self-assurance. You have to be feeling pretty good about yourself to dish out praise well in advance. If you doubt yourself, you'll doubt them. If you doubt them, you'll not praise them because you'll be sure they are going to screw up.

It takes nothing except courage to say, "Come on; you can do it. You'll be fine." The more responsibility you give people, the more you trust them, the more you praise them, the more you encourage them, the more they'll give you in return. Praise costs nothing and brings in loads. Encouragement should be a given.

Encourage an atmosphere where everyone encourages everyone else—"You can do it" should be heard every day all around you. If you're not saying it, chances are your team isn't either. Encourage the good ones to give the less good ones a hand up. In any good team an air of fostering help should be actively encouraged and praised when it happens. We're all in this together, and we sink or swim together.

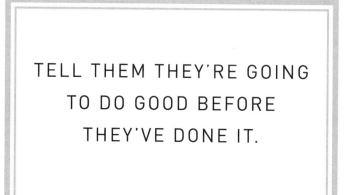

TELL THEM THEY'RE GOING
TO DO GOOD BEFORE
THEY'VE DONE IT.

Be Very, Very Good at Finding the Right People

You have to be good at finding the right people to fill the right jobs—and then leave them to get on with it. OK, I know this is one rule that requires a certain intuitive touch, but I'm sure you know the sort of manager I'm talking about. They seem to surround themselves with capable, competent people, and then they just seem to sit back and watch them go for gold. You can do that, too. It is a special talent but one you can cultivate. I guess the skill is in both picking the right people and letting go—leaving them alone to get on with it. You have to have lots of trust to do that; trust in their ability and trust in your own as well.

You have to have a very clear idea of who you are looking for to fill a job as much as what you are looking for. For instance, you might need a senior account manager—that is what you are looking for. But who? Team player? Good all rounder? Someone able to make decisions on the run? Someone who can plan ahead? Someone who understands your industry's quirks? Someone who speaks fluent spreadsheets? Someone who can work with an overexcitable union?

I'm sure you get the idea. If you have a clear picture of who you need as well as what you need, you make the transition to being a manager who seems to have an uncanny knack of finding the right people. It's not a knack, of course, but planning, vision, logic, and hard work.

I once made the mistake of being totally seduced by a manager's credentials—I was a general manager seeking to employ a manager—and failing to look hard enough at who he was rather than what he was. Yes, he had the credentials and was very good at his job. But he wasn't a team player and saw everything as a competition, mainly between him and the other managers. Fine in itself, but it didn't work for me or the other managers, who all wanted to pull together. This was one case where I was not good at finding the right person. I had found the wrong person, and it took a lot to extricate myself. I had only myself to blame because I hadn't thought sufficiently about who I wanted.

If you're not good at this, or think you could improve, invite somebody you respect to sit in on interviews with you to give you another perspective. Find a mentor or coach to help you work out who you really need.

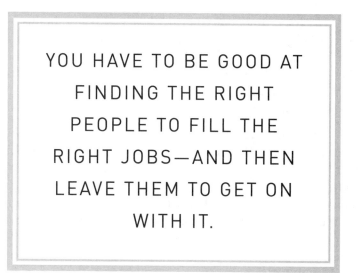

YOU HAVE TO BE GOOD AT FINDING THE RIGHT PEOPLE TO FILL THE RIGHT JOBS—AND THEN LEAVE THEM TO GET ON WITH IT.

RULE 16

Hire Raw Talent

Do you know how many publishers turned down the first *Harry Potter* book? I've heard several numbers quoted, but the answer is at least eight, whoever you ask. And what does that say about Barry Cunningham, the publisher who finally signed up the author? To just about everyone it says he was a whole lot smarter than all the folks who turned the book down.

All hugely successful managers were once fresh out of school or college, waiting for someone to recognize their talent and offer them a job. They were junior managers looking for promotion, or middle managers hoping it would be them who'd be asked to head up the new project or department or enterprise.

These are the people you want on your team. The raw talent, ready to step up. Never mind about experience—anyone can get that, given time. But you can't fake real talent, brains, and energy. When you find someone who has that, offer them the job first and worry about the details later. I'm not talking about mere enthusiasm—sadly lots of untalented people have that—but real ability and an intelligent grasp of the issues they'll be dealing with.

Of course, these talented recruits could eventually outshine you. They could fly up the career ladder and even overtake you. That worries some people. A lot. But it doesn't worry a Rules player. You see, Rules players understand that if it says anything about them at all, it will be reflected glory that shines on them. Just like the publisher who offered JK Rowling her first contract.

Think about it. These people are going to get to the top with or without you. How much better to be the one who had the perception to recognize them, and the sense to hire them, and the privilege to set them on their upward way.

After you start putting your own team together, the people in it and their performance says more about you as a manager than anything else does. The better the team, the more impressed people will be with you. Hell, some top managers will confess to you that their only real talent has been in hiring people who were smarter than them. They may say it self-deferentially, but actually it's really the only skill you need to get to the top. Know who to hire, and then stay out of their way except to give them what they need to do the job. That doesn't make you a bad manager, it makes you a top class one, because your team will outperform the rest thanks to your talent-spotting skills.

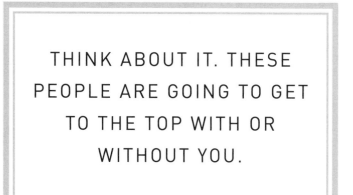

THINK ABOUT IT. THESE PEOPLE ARE GOING TO GET TO THE TOP WITH OR WITHOUT YOU.

RULE 17

Take the Rap

Sorry, but if the team screws up, it is entirely your fault. If the team does well, the credit is all theirs. A good manager will always take the rap. I know it's easy to use your team as an excuse, but it won't wash. You are the leader, the manager, the boss. If it all goes bottoms up, you have to stand up and take the flack.

It is very easy to say, "We didn't meet our targets because…." But you have to say, "I didn't meet my targets because…." And that "because" has to be followed by "I," never "they."

It is easy to say, "We didn't meet our targets because young Brian accidentally upset Client X, and they pulled out leaving us short of our sales." But who put young Brian in charge of such an important client? You. Who organized the sale? You. It has to be you. And your team will die for you if you ask it to, if you take the rap when the going gets tough, believe me. Nothing generates more loyalty than a boss who's prepared to stand up and say, "I take responsibility."

But I also know this is a tough one, really tough to do. It takes self-confidence, courage, trust (that you won't get sacked or disciplined) and a certain maturity.

You might think it will go against you, look as if you are incompetent, but on the contrary. If your boss sees you stand up and say, "We lost the contract and I take responsibility—these are the steps we're taking to make sure it doesn't happen again," they won't see a failure—they will see a future board member.

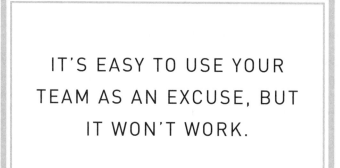

IT'S EASY TO USE YOUR
TEAM AS AN EXCUSE, BUT
IT WON'T WORK.

RULE 18

Give Credit to the Team When It Deserves It

Just as you must always stand up and take the blame, so too must you always heap praise and credit on your team when things go well. If that fabulous sale to Client X comes off because you happened to stay up all night working on it and then used an old contact from a previous job and then swung it because you happened to know something the competition didn't—why, then you say, "The team did it."

Taking the blame does generate loads of loyalty, but so too does giving the team the credit. Say it loudly, in public, sincerely, but do say it. And don't do it tongue in cheek with "My team did it," as if you are giving it credit but making sure everyone knows who really was responsible. The implication that it is your team isn't necessary. Everyone knows it is your team so there is no need to mention it, ever. It is OK to say, "It did a great job; it is a fantastic team. I'm incredibly lucky to have it." This implies you had nothing to do with it, and yet everyone knows it is your team and you are its leader, so the team will love you, and everyone else will think you incredibly humble and self-effacing. Well done you.

Again, all this takes courage and a lot of self-confidence, I know. You work hard, and it doesn't seem fair to give the credit away. I know that you really want to stand up and shout, "Look, it was me, I did this, all by myself, OK?" But you can't.

You see, you didn't do it all by yourself, no matter how much you might believe that. If you are selling, then it is the team that built the product you are selling. Without that team you would have nothing to sell. Tell the team that selling the product was a breeze because it had done such a good job. It will glow with pride and redouble its efforts.

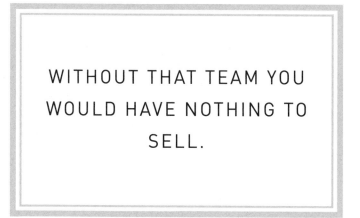

WITHOUT THAT TEAM YOU
WOULD HAVE NOTHING TO
SELL.

RULE 19

Get the Best Resources for Your Team

If your team is a tool you use to get greater glory for little ol' you, then the resources your team uses are the tools it needs to carry it—and thus you—onward and forward. Too many managers think that by cutting their team's resources they are earning some sort of brownie points to be stored up—and used in what? Heaven? I don't think so. You have to get the best resources for your team. By depriving the team you are depriving it also of the chance to shine, to propel you to greater glory.

I know of a lot of managers who say, "Oh, they can manage for a few more years with Windows Vista." Or "They'd probably just play games all day with a new iPhone; I can save a buck or two if I hold off for a bit." I have even heard, "I try to keep a short rein on what they need in case it gets out of hand."

For heaven's sake. Get your team the best, the very, very best, and then let it get on with its job—which is to make you look good.

If your people need technology—get it for them even if you have to move heaven and earth. If they need more staff, paper stuff, bigger and better machines, higher quality tools—go get 'em. Whatever it is they need to get their job done slicker, quicker, better, bigger, faster, more productively, cheaper, whatever—go get it. If you have to argue, sweat blood, plead, beg, or bust a budget or two—do it. Do it now.

You simply can't expect your team to a) give of their best or b) be motivated, if you fail them. They will talk to other people you know: colleagues in the same organization, friends in other organizations. They will know when they are being short-changed and they will resent it, resent you, and work less effectively. As a result, you will fail to shine. *Ipso facto*—go get them the best you can.

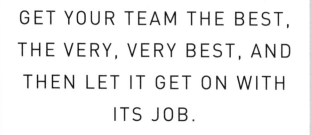

GET YOUR TEAM THE BEST, THE VERY, VERY BEST, AND THEN LET IT GET ON WITH ITS JOB.

RULE 20

Celebrate

I find an excuse every day to reward my staff with a little something—a modest celebration for a result no matter how small, how trivial it seems. If you do the same, you'll have a motivated staff who have a habit of celebrating every success. And that's so important.

And the rewards? Tiny. A box of doughnuts. Extra froth on their cappuccinos. A chance to go outside and sit in the sun.

Sometimes I declare today a special day because we just got such and such a result, and then I take them out to lunch, let them take time off, let them tell me their worst jokes—never all at the same time, mind.

And, occasionally, I declare such a special day even if we fail to win an order. I reward mistakes, screw-ups, failures, accidents. Why? Well, they've all done their best, given their all, and sweated blood. Why shouldn't I reward them? Just because we failed doesn't mean we didn't strive. I am rewarding the effort. I am celebrating all that we did right—effort, struggle, determination, teamwork, drive, and good honest labor.

Don't just celebrate the big wins; celebrate all the little ones as well—obviously with smaller celebrations, but celebrations of some sort nevertheless. Hey, any excuse to go and get a coffee. And a bag of doughnuts (or apples if they like). What does that cost you? Very little, but the warm feeling it generates far exceeds any cost.

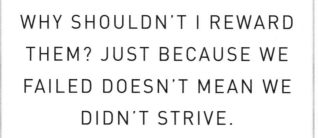

WHY SHOULDN'T I REWARD THEM? JUST BECAUSE WE FAILED DOESN'T MEAN WE DIDN'T STRIVE.

RULE 21

Keep Track of Everything You Do and Say

Now why would you want to do this, unless you're up to no good? No, quite the reverse in fact. The better a manager you are, the more information you need to keep. Why? Two reasons.

First, consistency. You need to keep everything because you will need to check back from time to time. The question, "Now how did I do this before?" will crop up constantly. Your team needs you to be consistent, and you can't be that if you don't remember what you did last time.

If Jim won that big contract last time and you gave him a catered lunch and then Terri pulls off a similar deal and you take her out for coffee and a bagel, chances are she's not going to be happy and next time won't give you her very best. So write it down and check back. Similarly if you tell Client X that they are getting the same deal as Client Y, and then they discover that's not true, they will probably take their business elsewhere. Be consistent.

Second, proof. Being a good manager, a damn good manager, may open you up to jealousy, resentment, and distrust. Not everybody is as upfront as you.

If your team is giving you 110 percent and someone else's is only giving them 60 percent because they are a bad manager, the chances are they will think you're up to something rather than looking at their own poor mismanagement skills. It just might be useful to show where successful projects originated, or that you did everything you said you would.

Decisions have to be taken, memos sent, emails written, and reports presented. Just keep a record of everything. All emails should be saved: this is no big deal because computer storage is so immense these days that if all the emails ever sent were saved, it would still only fill a cyber-tea cup.

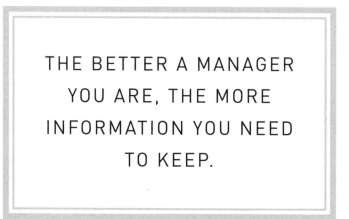

THE BETTER A MANAGER
YOU ARE, THE MORE
INFORMATION YOU NEED
TO KEEP.

Be Sensitive to Friction

When you are running a team, you are dealing with people. And sometimes they take it into their heads to rub each other the wrong way. Why? Who knows. They just do. They encroach on each other's space, eat each other's lunches, take each other's parking spaces. Who starts it? Who knows. Can you let it go on? The hell you can. It has to be nipped in the bud.

You have to be sensitive to friction almost before it begins— and do something about it. There is no point letting it go on for a day longer than it needs to. But to do this you really do need to be on the ball. You have to know your team very well indeed to spot those first early warning signs.

If you don't nip it in the bud, it will grow into a monster. From tiny nit-picking you'll end up with a full-scale war, with the rest of the team taking sides.

What to look out for? Silences when there shouldn't be. Odd complaints, "I wish Clare would stop nagging to me so much." Grumblings and bitchy gossip. Fierce competitiveness where there doesn't need to be any. Sudden appearance of demarcation lines, such as potted plants to desk screens. Books or computers on desks being used to screen or shield people. People being left out of social invites. People being left out of office humor.

I'm sure you know as much about this as I do and keep your eyes open and your ear to the ground. The secret is stopping it before it gets too bad. Here you have to be diplomat, parent, politician, and referee.

You mustn't be seen to be taking sides. You must be seen to be taking swift and resolute action, making it clear that feuding won't be tolerated. Call them in. Reason with them. Separate them. Swap their shifts. Keep them apart. Make them work together as a partnership. There are a whole lot of things you can do, and I'm sure you'll pick the right one at the right time for the right situation.

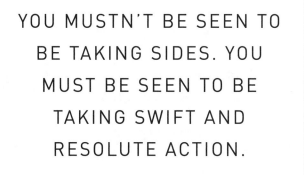

YOU MUSTN'T BE SEEN TO BE TAKING SIDES. YOU MUST BE SEEN TO BE TAKING SWIFT AND RESOLUTE ACTION.

Create a Good Atmosphere

Creating a good atmosphere isn't only easy but also essential. If your staff are sullen and despondent and depressed and surly—it shows. It shows in their work, the way they handle customers and colleagues, the way they relate to each other, and most important the way they work with you and for you.

It takes nothing to say good morning politely and mean it. It isn't a chore to make sure everyone has got coffee or tea for a meeting. It takes a second to ask, "How are you today?" The three rules for any workplace are

- Politeness
- Friendliness
- Kindness

Yep, we've all known the bosses who shout and are rude and belligerent, but, like the dinosaurs, they are a dying breed, and we can move on. People are entitled to

- Respect
- Civilized behavior
- Dignity

If you can't give them these things you shouldn't be a manager. But I'm sure you can. Creating a good atmosphere is easy. It comes from the top down. It is your job and your responsibility to be cheerful, considerate, polite, and helpful. Your people are one of your most important resources—your tools, your weapons of mass achievement. Without them you are nothing. With them you are a team. Use them kindly and don't abuse them. Be genuinely interested in them and their lives. If you don't have time—make time.

I guess the word I am looking for is courtesy. An old-fashioned concept, I'll grant you, but one that gets mountains moved, doors opened, and staff working shifts they would normally have refused to do.

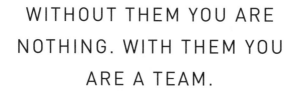

WITHOUT THEM YOU ARE
NOTHING. WITH THEM YOU
ARE A TEAM.

RULE 24

Inspire Loyalty and Team Spirit

If you work together, chances are you are seeing more of your team than you are of your family. And your team is seeing more of you than of their families. If this is the case you had better all get along. Now you don't have to love each other, but you do have to be a family. And the best way to do that is to inspire loyalty and create a team spirit. You, as the manager, have to be the head of the family.

You have to be respected, looked up to, trusted, and relied upon. Tall order. Strong stuff. Can you do all that? Course you can. All you have to do is

- Reward them
- Praise them
- Be kind to them
- Trust them
- Inspire them
- Lead them
- Motivate them
- Grow them
- Genuinely care about them

These are the kinds of things that are easier to say than to do, and there's a temptation for you to skip down the list saying "Yes, yes, I do that." Now take a minute and go back and really think about each one. Do you *really* do that? Could you do it better? Are you absolutely sure you *think* you do it, but perhaps don't actually do it? What people think they do and what they actually do can be very different indeed. Find somebody you can ask for honest feedback. Ideally one of your team—if not, somebody who sees you with your team. What do they say you do?

I once worked in competition with another company. One of that manager's team lived with one of my team. She told John, my team member, all her boss's plans, figures, results, future promotions, and so on, and I was able to beat him every time. Now why didn't she pass on all my stuff to her boss, seeing as she obviously discussed work with John? Simple. She didn't like her manager. And that was his fault entirely. He was rude to his staff, abusive, uncooperative, and unkind. Was I a soft touch? No way. I was strict and businesslike, but I treated my team with respect. I didn't have to do much because my competitor was doing enough wrong to make me look good.

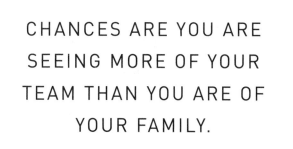

CHANCES ARE YOU ARE
SEEING MORE OF YOUR
TEAM THAN YOU ARE OF
YOUR FAMILY.

Have and Show Trust in Your Staff

You have a computer I take it? OK, it crashes from time to time—that's a given. You have a car. It breaks down from time to time—that, too, is a given. Now you don't eye either of these warily, expecting them to let you down, watching them like a hawk in case they show any sign of breaking down, do you? No, of course not. So stop watching your staff like that. They are a tool to getting a job done. They will break down, crash, whatever, from time to time, but we accept their limitations—Rule 13—and we allow them to make mistakes—Rule 12—and we accept that we aren't managing them but their processes instead.

And if you can make that move to trusting your staff, you must show them that you are doing exactly that. Trust not only has to be done, but it also has to be seen to be done. Sometimes you'll have to make a big show of really leaving them alone to get on with it.

You show them that you trust them by backing off, leaving them alone to get on with the job. Stop peering over their shoulders, checking every few moments, looking up nervously every time they move or cough or get up. Relax and let them get on with it. You can still ask them to report back at the end of the day/week and encourage them to come to you to discuss any problems. Just make it clear you trust them to do it, and you are always there if they need support or guidance.

But, I hear you say, what if I really don't trust them? What if I know they're a lazy, good-for-nothing, shiftless bunch of liberty takers? What if, indeed? Whose team is it? Who employed, trained, kept such a bunch of monkeys?

Sorry, bit harsh, but sometimes we need to face the reality. If you can't trust your team, you need to look to your own management skills—or keep reading. A good team leader (that's you) has a good team following them. If the team is faulty, then the leadership has to be challenged—that's not going to be you. If the team is right, you can trust them. If the team really can't be trusted (and are you sure about that?) then it needs to be changed.

> YOU SHOW THEM THAT YOU TRUST THEM BY BACKING OFF, LEAVING THEM ALONE TO GET ON WITH THE JOB.

RULE 26

Respect Individual Differences

I have several children. I expect them to operate as a team. But I am also shrewd enough to realize they are all completely different, and if I try to treat them all the same, apply the same rules—apart from the discipline ones—I'll get a mutiny, or chaos. Now one of them—and I'm not mentioning any names here but they will know which one I'm talking about—can't be hurried. Not ever, not anyhow. If you shove, he digs his heels in and can't be shifted. He has to be lured, enticed, and seduced into being quicker. But I have another son who constantly has to be slowed down. I have to respect—and work with—their individual differences. I simply have to.

Now your team is just the same. Some members can be hurried and others can't. Some will need to be slowed down and others you need to speed up. Some will come to work with a cheery smile, others are best not approached first thing in the morning. Some will be terribly good with technology and others won't. Go back to what Belbin says in Rule 2 and see how everybody in a team has something different to offer—and that difference is what makes your team superb.

With my children if I need something done fast, I know who to call on. If I need a slower, more methodical approach, I select another child.

You don't have to let anyone get away with anything just because they are different—keep the discipline rules in place—it's more in the way you treat individual differences, the way you select tasks, and the way you expect those tasks to be carried out. We are all different, thank goodness—a world populated by people like me, even I realize, would be ghastly—and those differences are what make a great team pull together effectively.

So if you're managing a sales team, say, and most of the members are sharp-suited and have slick patter (like you), but one prefers casual garb and is more chatty with his customers, don't mark his cards as "not a company man"—judge him on the results he gets. If he makes his targets and his customers love him, then *vive la différence*.

DIFFERENCES ARE WHAT
MAKE A GREAT TEAM PULL
TOGETHER EFFECTIVELY.

Listen to Ideas from Others

If you think you know it all, chances are you will be too busy listening to yourself and how great you are to have time to listen to anyone else. But I know that's not you. Everyone, no matter their position or rank, has something to offer you. Try talking to the lift operator, the car park attendant, the cleaning staff, whoever and whatever. And, most important, listen to people on your team. They are the ones in the know who have to work with the resources and the products. They are the ones at the cutting edge, and they may well have ideas, good ideas. You don't need to consult them over every little thing but the big things...well, yes. Talk to them. Get their feedback, their ideas, their creativity.

You obviously have to be careful to make sure that although you are listening to them it is you who still is in charge. You might listen but that doesn't mean you are going to act on every one of their ideas. Nip in the bud the feeling that if they suggest, you have to carry out. Therein lies terrible trouble. Listen, assimilate, and then decide based on what you've heard, your own experience and ideas, and what is practical. It's no good you listening and then not using their information and they becoming terribly despondent—"What's the use of telling the boss my ideas, they're never used."

You have to listen without giving the idea that you will necessarily use their ideas, so then they won't be disappointed when you do something completely different. But you can make them think their ideas were incorporated into your overall strategy.

Virtually every team member I have ever known could tell their manager something useful about what they as a team or a company are getting wrong, or how something could be done better. If you're open to this, ask good questions and listen without prejudice (or talking over them), you're immediately in a different class than most managers.

TALK TO THEM. GET THEIR
FEEDBACK, THEIR IDEAS,
THEIR CREATIVITY.

RULE 28

Adapt Your Style to Each Team Member

Adapting your style does not mean you have to be a chameleon. It means you have to be sensitive to your team's individuality and work with it. You may have outgoing members who like to be praised in public, and then you might have quieter, more introspective members who would shrivel up and die if praised in public and prefer to be told they are doing a good job privately. There, you've changed your style without changing your skin, spots, or personality.

I have one team member, a very good one, who does her job superbly but who absolutely hates appraisals and would do anything to get out of them. She loathes having to talk about herself in any way—and this borders almost on a real phobia. I have to change my style with her considerably when carrying out a six-monthly appraisal because if she gets wind of the fact that I'm even thinking about doing one she'll hyperventilate and have a panic attack. And then I have another team member who greets me each morning with a very cheery, "How am I doing, Boss?" Now he really likes talking about himself and would happily be given a daily appraisal—if I were to let it happen. Both team members do their job extremely well—they wouldn't be there if they didn't—but they do need handling in a completely different way. I want them both to continue doing good work, and I have to handle them differently to get the best from them.

Similarly, some people like to be left alone, to create opportunities and make things happen, and they will come and tell you if they need help (the bright self-motivators) and others will need you to direct their actions more and give them specific projects to do. Don't overmanage the former—they'll resist and they'll get irritated (and quite possibly leave). Equally, don't under-manage the latter or they will feel stressed by a lack of structure to their job and won't work hard. Think about the individual. Think about what they need and what motivates them, and adapt your management style accordingly.

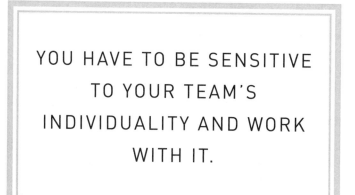

YOU HAVE TO BE SENSITIVE TO YOUR TEAM'S INDIVIDUALITY AND WORK WITH IT.

RULE 29

Let Them Think They Know More Than You (Even if They Don't)

This one is so simple, and yet I bet very few managers use it. And why not? It makes people feel really special and important. All you have to do is say to your staff, "You know about this, what do you think?" The key principles to this rule are

- Ask their opinion.
- Get their ideas and views.
- Give them more responsibility than they ever had before—you'll be surprised how people always rise to a challenge.
- Discuss important issues and news with them.
- Encourage feedback.
- Never dismiss them as being "mere workers."

Even if you *know* you know more about a subject than they do—still do it. They feel good. They perform better. They learn from your conversations. Maybe you learn, too.

And while you're doing all this, take them through the entire process of your industry so that they don't get stuck in a rut of one department. You have to let them see their important role in the overall scheme of things, how their contribution is valuable and helpful, and how the whole thing would flounder without them.

Treat them as you would a valuable client you were showing round. Let them in on your industry's secrets: "Well, we use the new XP8 coatings on our silicon chips, unlike Mathers and Crowley who still use the old XP5, but I expect you know that anyway, but do keep it under your hat as it's how we stole an idea from them and got that huge contract with the DVLA last year."

Keep them informed about developments in your industry—perhaps you could subscribe to your industry's newsletters and magazines, technical journals, and papers, that sort of thing—so that they think you are assuming they are interested, informed, and know more than perhaps they do. This will encourage them to keep learning and wanting to know more.

> ENCOURAGE THEM TO
> KEEP LEARNING AND
> WANTING TO KNOW MORE.

Don't Always Have to Have the Last Word

Yes, yes, I know you are the boss, the manager—and a damn good one, may I say—but you don't always have to have the last word. This isn't like being kids on the playground.

If people in your team disagree with you openly, then there are two possible reasons why: Either they feel confident enough to engage in debate (in which case you ought to appreciate that) or they are out of line, and you aren't imposing discipline enough to stop them. It may well be a warning sign that things are wrong or a sign that things are very right—only you can judge.

If they are out of line and there's a discipline issue, obviously you need to deal with that in private. Otherwise, remember that your staff is composed of grown-ups. You have to give them room to be real people, and that means they will sometimes disagree, argue, and get mad. That's fine on a good team where people can sound off and nobody takes umbrage. It obviously doesn't work in a poor team.

It doesn't pay always to have the last word or always to be right or always to correct staff on every little thing. Sometimes, whether they are right or wrong, it's best to let it go. Know the difference between things important enough that you need to have the last word, and things where it really doesn't matter.

> REMEMBER THAT YOUR STAFF IS COMPOSED OF GROWN-UPS. YOU HAVE TO GIVE THEM ROOM TO BE REAL PEOPLE.

RULE 31

Understand the Roles of Others

I used to believe that to be a good manager I had to be able to do not only my own job—managing—but also everyone else's job as well. And probably, I thought in my heart of hearts, I should be able to do it as well as them if not better. Thus, I figured, if there was an emergency I could step in and do their job and everything would carry on functioning. Yep, I bet you're there before me. If I were to step into their job, who would be doing mine?

Answer, of course: nobody.

The key is to have a practical understanding of what all the jobs entail but realize that you don't need to be able actually to do them. Yes, you do need back-up in the event of a crisis, but it ain't you. You're better off right where you are—managing.

To understand the role, the best way is to know what problems it solves and how it works. But you don't need to be able to do it as well as your team member does—that's what you pay them for. Something about keeping dogs and barking yourself—you need to know what job the guard dog does, but you don't need to go round biting burglars to appreciate it fully.

And often you'll employ someone for such a specialized job you wouldn't know where to begin. You might be the manager of a power plant, but you don't need to know how to calculate the shelf life of plutonium. But you do need to know that you employ someone who can do that job for you.

It's also important for all your team to have an understanding of what everyone else does. This certainly helps create a team spirit and a sense of loyalty.

> YOU DON'T NEED TO BE
> ABLE TO DO A ROLE AS
> WELL AS YOUR TEAM
> MEMBER DOES—THAT'S
> WHAT YOU PAY THEM FOR.

RULE 32

Ensure People Know Exactly What Is Expected of Them

It's easy to give someone a job description and a contract and then sit back and expect them to get on with it. Trouble is, it leads to a lot of confused people and wasted time. Better to let them know right from the start what is expected of them.

And what is expected of them? Well, it's a whole lot more than just the job itself. You have to think through every individual role and what exactly is expected of that person.

It's vital that people know what part they play in any strategic plan and what is expected of them as a result. It's essential that team members know the values and standards of the team and the company, and what's expected of them in attitude and behavior (open? honest? imaginative? caring? can do?). It's also about them being clear on emotional requirements, punctuality, working overtime, behavior toward colleagues, crisis management—everything.

For new employees this is helped if you have a "buddy" program where each new person is linked to someone more experienced who can show them the ropes.

Oh, and some guidelines on relationships at work. It's only fair that everyone knows what is expected of them in any given situation—you can't discipline someone for having sex in the broom closet if it hasn't been spelled out to them that they don't do that sort of thing—"But we always did it at my previous place of work and no one complained."

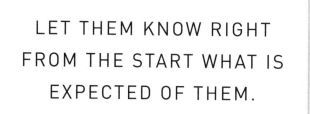

LET THEM KNOW RIGHT
FROM THE START WHAT IS
EXPECTED OF THEM.

Have Clear Expectations

One manager I worked with was very moody. When she was relaxed, everyone was productive but had fun. Occasional pranks kept their spirits up, and she didn't have a problem with it, in moderation. When she was stressed, however, you could get your head bitten off for as little as laughing too loud.

As I say, there were times she was very relaxed. But no one else on her team was. They had no idea what mood she'd be in, so they were always on edge. Would she be happy with a report that was poorly presented but contained all the facts, or would she rather wait until tomorrow and have it looking perfect? Could you get away with the briefest of paperwork for a particular procedure, or did you need to fill it in in triplicate, dotting every i and crossing every t? Hard to say really—it depended which side of bed she got out of that morning.

And how did her team respond? Well, if you've ever worked for a manager like that, you'll know the answer. They were pretty demoralized, and their standards were hugely inconsistent. Obviously, because their manager's standards were similarly wide-ranging.

Look, if your team doesn't know what your standards are, how can they aspire to them? They're looking to you to set the lead, and if you don't, they can't tell where they're going or how they're supposed to get there. You have to be consistent in the standards you set and the performance you expect. If something is unacceptable on Monday at 10 a.m., it should be unacceptable on Friday at 4 p.m. If paperwork is supposed to be filled out a particular way, that's the way it should be done every day of the week.

It may sound unreasonable to have a basic standard and then suddenly, for no consistent reason, to expect more of people. And so it is. But it's just as unfair to let them get away with less just because you're in a particular mood. You're not being nice to them—you're confusing them. And you're failing to ensure your team always produces work of the highest standard. And how fair is it to let one person get away with a scrappy presentation when their colleague was expected to produce a polished document last week? No, the only way to ensure good morale among your team, and to make sure it turns in a consistently strong performance, is for you to be consistent in enforcing the standards that you set.

And if you ask me next week, I'll tell you exactly the same.

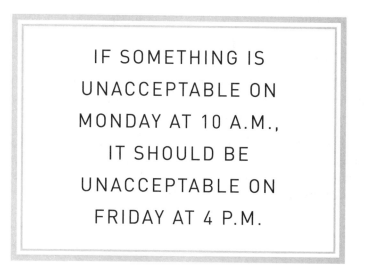

IF SOMETHING IS
UNACCEPTABLE ON
MONDAY AT 10 A.M.,
IT SHOULD BE
UNACCEPTABLE ON
FRIDAY AT 4 P.M.

RULE 34

Use Positive Reinforcement Motivation

If your staff does something good, tell them. And then tell them again. And again. Keep it up. Put it in writing. Send them a memo—something they can keep. Put it in the company newsletter. Add a note to their file. Whatever, but make it widely known they did good. This is a quick—and cheap (important, with your limited budget)—method of praising and motivating your team (and individual members of course) and it lets everyone know you are monitoring, praising, and motivating.

When you praise people, make it simple. If they worked late to get a special order out, say, "Thank you for working late, we couldn't have done it without you. Your positive response to a difficult situation made everyone's job (especially mine) a lot easier. Thank you."* That's a whole lot easier than, "On the evening of the 7th you were asked to implement an extra shift duty, which you carried out in accordance with our wishes and for which we wish to convey our gratitude, blah, blah...."

Let them know why you are thanking them—*you made my job easier*—rather than just thanking them for what they did—*you came in for an extra shift*.

Be personal. Use "I" and "we," not "management." And say "thank you" in the same way as you would speak. "I want to thank you" is so much better than "The management wants to express its gratitude"—who speaks like that?

* Reinforce by saying *thank you* again.

Praise as soon as the job is done, not a week later—do it the next day at the latest. And do it every time people do something beyond their normal brief. If they are asked to work an extra shift every week, that is just a part of their normal working pattern; instead, we are talking here of the extraordinary, the beyond the normal, going that extra mile sort of stuff.

If you reinforce positive behavior in this way, you will almost certainly guarantee it happening again. Fail to notice, to comment, to praise, and chances are your team will stop giving you their best—and who can blame them?

WHEN YOU PRAISE PEOPLE, MAKE IT SIMPLE.

RULE 35

Don't Try Justifying Stupid Systems

I was traveling on the subway the other day when we encountered a problem. It was fairly simple. Someone had messed with a security door and triggered an alarm—or something. This brought the train to a standstill, probably quite rightly. But it did this in a very long tunnel. The train couldn't move until the fault had been rectified, which involved finding the train manager and getting him to reset the triggered alarm. All fairly simple.

I was running very late for a meeting, so asked if there wasn't a better system. The train manager spent about 20 minutes justifying why this system was the best for everyone concerned, him, staff, train authorities, everyone that is except me, the poor passenger. Much better if he'd just said, "Yes, it's a useless system and I shall recommend we change it; thank you for your concern."

And I bet you have a dozen useless systems within your organization—we all do. Best not try to justify them. If you can't change them, put up with it, get on with it, but don't try tricking the staff into thinking it's all fabulous. It isn't, and you lose respect and trust if you try convincing people that it's fine when they know it's not.

I'm not saying you should go round lamenting loudly every-thing that is bad about your company—far from it, that road leads only to ruin. Remember, if you can't say something nice, don't say anything at all. Just don't try justifying something you know is stupid, especially to your team.

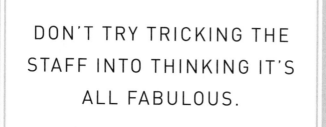

DON'T TRY TRICKING THE
STAFF INTO THINKING IT'S
ALL FABULOUS.

Be Ready to Say Yes

The good manager—that's you—tries to stay completely fresh. Not to get stuck in the same old ways of doing things. That means not having a default mechanism of "No, we don't do it like that." Instead replace it with "That's an interesting idea. How do you think that would work?"

What's more, you need to encourage people to come up with new ideas, as well as coming up with them yourself. Try ideas out. Take one new idea each week and try it. It might be fairly simple, "We'd like more choice of muffins with our morning coffee, please," or something radical, "Listen up, guys, we're going to try a completely new approach to sales and distribution."

Obviously it makes sense to try out smaller ideas first to make sure your team can cope well with change, and then move on to the more radical ones later. Break 'em in slowly.

And as fast as you are introducing new ideas, get your team to do the same with their own individual jobs so that they don't grow stale either. If everyone has a new idea each week, that's a huge number of new ideas by the end of the year for themselves and for the whole team. "I just thought I could speed the process up if I...." "Wow, I could take that idea and adapt it to my work station and then I could...." "Yeah, and I bet they'd be really interested in this in accounts because it could speed up the whole...." And so on.

Biggest challenge? Getting your team on board—everyone is resistant to change initially. If you waiver, the whole team will also waiver. If you maintain the passion, the whole team will be infected and become addicted to this. Believe me. Trust me. I know you already have enough to do, but we'll move on to delegating in a bit and that'll free up some time. Then you'll have more time to do this, which, in a way, is part of your real job—managing.

Encourage innovation. Reward good ideas. Create a culture where ideas are recognized (even if not adopted) and valued.

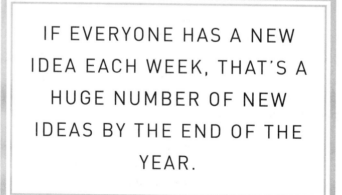

IF EVERYONE HAS A NEW IDEA EACH WEEK, THAT'S A HUGE NUMBER OF NEW IDEAS BY THE END OF THE YEAR.

RULE 37

Train Them to Bring You Solutions, Not Problems

It's too easy for staff to moan. I think it becomes a habit. You have to train your staff not just to moan. You can allow moaning but insist that if they bring you a problem they must also suggest a solution to the problem. Any idea that there is something wrong should always be met with, "And what would you like me to do about it?" If they complain, meet them with, "What do you think we should do?"

The best manager I ever worked for carried this even further and made us tell him the solution first—and then let him guess what he thought our "problem" was. It made it a game, which was sort of fun, but it also made us think on our feet a bit—made us be a bit lateral in our moaning. I was having a problem with security staff. I thought they were erasing the CCTV footage without watching it, which was not on. This was my problem because if anything had happened, I would have been blamed. I needed them to watch carefully but couldn't devise a solution to this problem—but I couldn't just go to the boss and moan that they weren't doing their job properly. I had to come up with a solution first.

Then it dawned on me that I didn't need to go to the boss. I could solve this one myself. I had to make sure the security staff thought there was something worth watching. I mentioned that some members of staff had been reported as having sex somewhere on the premises, and it could have been covered by the CCTV cameras, but no one was sure by which camera. There were cameras covering car parks, offices, hallways, and storage areas in the basement. Result. The security folks started watching as if their lives depended on it. My boss was pleased because this was part of my job description, and he had noticed it wasn't being done properly and was going to call me out on it. And I had come up with a solution to a problem without going to my boss and just moaning, "Oh, the security people aren't doing their job properly...."

Admittedly I had to come up with a fresh solution once the security staff realized they weren't going to see any smutty pictures—but it took them a long time, and they kept going back just in case....

ANY IDEA THAT THERE IS
SOMETHING WRONG
SHOULD ALWAYS BE
MET WITH,
"AND WHAT WOULD YOU
LIKE ME TO DO ABOUT IT?"

PART II

MANAGING YOURSELF

So that's the basic rules for managing a team. And obviously most managers have a team to manage. But all managers have themselves to manage as well—that's you. So the next set of rules is for you. These are rules to help you become more effective as well as more efficient. It's hard enough just getting through the day without trying to improve as well, believe me I know.

Being a manager is a tough job because it is always two jobs at once. You have to get your own work done and also be looking out for a team. The higher up the scale we go, the further away from our original job we get. And often no one bothers to train us as to what the new job—management—actually entails. Sure we take the odd course—and some are very odd: I speak as one who has made LEGO® bridges, done jigsaw puzzles that are face down, been on canoeing weekends and all in the name of management training—but we don't specifically train to be managers. Management is something we sort of pick up as we go along. Sure there are a few good instinctive man-agers, but invariably we stumble along picking up the odd hint and clue here and there—it's a very hit and miss operation.

And a lot of what we are taught is fairly obvious. What I'm doing here is giving you the unwritten stuff—the stuff you don't get on those canoeing weekends.

RULE 38

Work Hard

The fundamental Rule of Management, I'm afraid, is get the basic job done, get it done well, and work extremely hard at it. No good being a fantastic people manager if you let the basic job slip. You may have to get into the office earlier than anyone else, earlier than you've ever arrived there before, but get in early you must.

After you have cleared your work out of the way, you can concentrate on managing your team. Paperwork has to be done efficiently and on time. This isn't the place to go into lengthy training sessions on time management and the like, but basically you will have to be

- Organized
- Dedicated
- Ruthlessly efficient
- Focused

No choice I'm afraid. You have to buckle down and just do it. Management isn't running around issuing orders and looking cool. It's actually about what goes on in the background—the work being done where no one sees it.

And if you want to know if you are being a good manager now—take a look at your desk. Go on. Right now. What do you see? Clear space and order? Paper everywhere and piles of unsorted stuff? Do the same with your briefcase, files, computer even. Order or disorder?

You have to use whatever tools you have at hand to make sure the work is done, done well, and done on time. Make lists, use pop-up calendars on your computer, delegate, seek help, stay up late, get up early, get up earlier—obviously you still need to refer to Rule 75: Go home; you have to have a life. But get that work done and learn to be ruthlessly efficient.

> YOU HAVE TO BUCKLE
> DOWN AND JUST DO IT.

RULE 39

Set the Standard

If you drag in late, argue with your customers, are disrespectful and produce shoddy work, chances are your team is going to go to hell in a hand basket. If, on the other hand, and I assume this is more likely the case, you arrive not only on time but also early, do your work well and on time (see Rule 38), behave like a decent, honest, civilized human being, and use your talent, chances are your staff will arise to the occasion.

Everyone needs someone to look up to, someone they can respect and want to emulate. Sorry, but that someone is you. Tough call I know. If you think heroes are so out of date, old-fashioned and redundant, then think again. Every one on your team has a special relationship with you. You are their leader, their inspiration, their boss (there's a word to make you shudder, but that's what you are), their mentor, guide, teacher, hero, role model, champion, defender, and guardian. To be all these things means you have to set an example. You have to play the part. You have to set standards. You have to be that role model.

The bottom line is: If you don't care, why should they? You've got to set an example in everything you do. Think before you speak. Consider how you react. "Do as I say, not as I do" doesn't work. Be what you want to see in them.

You've also got to go beyond that and raise their stakes. You've got to give your staff something to aspire to, something to want to raise themselves up to. That's you.

Ideally, you'll have some style, some flair, some spark of originality that will set you apart from the herd—we're thinking Lauren Bacall and Cary Grant here, not Meat Loaf and early Madonna.*

You've got to look the part, act the part, do the part—method acting here: Feel the manager, think the manager, be the manager.

YOU'VE GOT TO GIVE YOUR
STAFF SOMETHING TO
ASPIRE TO.

* No offense, both make really good albums and are superb rock stars but as role models for managers they don't cut the mustard.

RULE 40

Enjoy Yourself

I'm going to be blunt now. If you're not enjoying what you do, then get the hell out and make room for someone who is going to enjoy it. Rule 41 may put things into context, but for the moment we need to get you feeling good about what you're doing.

Enjoying work is about taking pleasure in a job well done, having an inner smile, finding something to laugh about, and not taking it too seriously. (No, this does not mean you laugh at people or fail to do your job to the very highest standards.)

Enjoying work is about seeing your job, your role, in a much bigger context. You can be hardworking and you can enjoy yourself—you can do both. You can be productive, effective, efficient, industrious, sober, reliable, and responsible—and yet still be having fun. It's your choice. No one told you that you had to be grave and uptight. All you were hired to do was your job.

The best thing is that if you learn when to be serious and when to let up and find humor in a situation, it will have a magical effect on those around you.

And if you work in a place where serious and uptight is the norm, here is a secret just for you: No one knows what is going on inside your head. No one. Just so long as the exterior is what they want, the inside can be whatever you want.

> NO ONE TOLD YOU
> THAT YOU HAD TO BE
> GRAVE AND UPTIGHT.
> ALL YOU WERE HIRED TO
> DO WAS YOUR JOB.

RULE 41

Don't Let It Get to You

If it all gets too much, remember it's just a job. Sure, one we care about and try to do to the very best of our ability. One we worry about and think about when we're not at work. One we would like to make better and improve and be more effective at.

But it is only a job when all is said and done.

Look around you. You'll see the ones who think that what they do is central to the Earth's movement or vital to the well-being of the entire planet. Nothing could be further from the truth. Enjoy it by all means. Take it seriously and give it all you've got, but remember it is just a job and it can be replaced, you can be replaced, the world will go on.

If the job is stressful in a way you don't like, think about something in life that is more important to you. Your kids, your dog, your mother. Your weekend hang-gliding trips. I don't know what you do when you're not at work, but find something that really matters, and use it to help you get through those bad times at work. Use it to get some perspective and recognize that there are more important things than your job.

You can even daydream about these important things to get you through the working day—so long as you promise you'll only do it when you're not supposed to be concentrating on the job. But meal breaks, walking over to another building, even when you go to the bathroom, are times you can stop for a moment and remind yourself of what matters in life.

And of course you should also spend time thinking about why work is getting you down, and come up with some kind of plan for improving things. Do you need to cut down your hours, resolve the festering feelings between team members, clinch a particular contract, or complete your next budget?

Well, get on with it if that's the case, and then you can get back to enjoying the job.

Not letting it get to you doesn't mean not caring or not taking pride and pleasure in what you do. No, it means putting things into context, so you can go home and switch off. Don't let it eat away at you, make you unhealthly, or stressed out.

> NOT LETTING IT GET TO YOU DOESN'T MEAN NOT CARING OR NOT TAKING PRIDE AND PLEASURE IN WHAT YOU DO.

RULE 42

Know What You Are Supposed to Be Doing

So what are you supposed to be doing? It's very easy to think you know, but do you really? It's like when your boss says, "I want this done as soon as possible." Now that's really easy; isn't it? Well, actually no. As soon as whose idea of possible? Yours? The boss's? And does "want" imply a wish or a need? And "done" is open to all sorts of interpretation.

I know I'm being picky and pedantic but I'm illustrating a point here. You know you have a team and you have to manage it. You know you have budgets and figures and targets and they all have to be met. You know you have a forward-looking strategy and you would like to implement that. You know you have a contract and a job description.

But what are you supposed to be doing? What's your priority? What's the end point? What's the goal? Has anything changed recently. (Senior management sometimes have a way of changing their minds and expecting you to know telepathically?)

I once worked for a senior manager who, to all outward appearances, wanted my team to be successful and productive but who seemed to be hampering my every move. Whenever I wanted to make changes that would drastically improve our figures, he hesitated and delayed and wouldn't make a decision. I couldn't figure out what I was supposed to be doing. I wanted to run the department for him as well as I could, but he seemed to be putting obstacles in my path.

Eventually I discovered that another department—run by a relative of his—was supposed to be the winning team. I wasn't allowed to be the golden boy because that was the role for his young nephew. He wanted me to fail so that young Sam could look good. I was supposed to be useless. When I had that info—what I was supposed to be doing—I could work effectively with it. You've got to know what you're supposed to be doing.

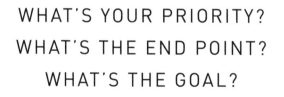

WHAT'S YOUR PRIORITY?
WHAT'S THE END POINT?
WHAT'S THE GOAL?

Know What You Are Actually Doing

So what are you doing? Important but overlooked rule, this one. Go on, answer the question, what are you doing?

To answer this you need to have long- and short-term plans form-ulated. If you haven't got a plan, you don't have a map. If you don't have a map, you'll never find the treasure. In Pirates of the Caribbean: The Curse of the Black Pearl, when someone questions his ability to sail his ship with only two men, Johnny Depp needs no other answer than he's Captain Jack Sparrow. "Savvy?" If you know who you are and where you are going, you are indeed a pirate and clearly so.

So, are you laying the groundwork for a future promotion? Marking time until you decide what to do? Counting down the days until you retire? Collecting information so you can go to a rival and use it profitably? Waiting to be head-hunted? Learning more about the industry so that you can make a lateral move? Enjoying yourself and having a ball? Doing a hatchet job for the management and making one-third of the workforce redundant?* Trying hard to be noticed by senior management? Working hard just to do a good job and stay ahead of the game? Building a social network to have fun with? Stealing ideas, resources, staff, and machinery to start your own rival business. (Oh, I've seen this done, and a very successful job they made of it, too—they knew exactly what they were actually doing.)

---

* I knew a general manager of a big engineering firm who was brought in to do exactly that—and the workforce knew it. His first mass meeting was greeted with boos and catcalls. He stood his ground and just said, "I am not the enemy here. The enemy is the downturn in business. I am not the enemy so don't shout at me." Worked like a charm.

There are no right and wrong answers. Well, actually a wrong answer would be, "I haven't a clue." You have to know what it is you are actually doing. Not what you are supposed to be doing. Not what you want to be doing. Not what the company thinks you are doing. But what you are actually doing. When you know that, you can work miracles because you have secret knowledge. Perhaps everyone else also knows; perhaps no one else knows. But you know and that is the important thing.

Now have a quick look at your team and tell me what every one is actually doing. Good exercise.

IF YOU HAVEN'T GOT A
PLAN, YOU DON'T HAVE A
MAP. IF YOU DON'T HAVE A
MAP, YOU'LL NEVER FIND
THE TREASURE.

RULE 44

Value Your Time

I once sat in a meeting, as a very junior manager, in which there was an interminable discussion going on about whether we should buy a particular piece of equipment that some people thought too pricey. I'd said what I had to say on the subject (as indeed had everyone, but some of them were saying it several times) so to pass the time I did a quick, back-of-the-envelope calculation of the combined hourly rate of everyone sitting round the table. I pretty much knew every-one's salaries, so it would have been a fairly close estimate. The interesting thing was that the half hour we spent talking about this piece of equipment was nearly twice as costly as the thing itself.

As a Rules manager, you need to know what your time is worth, and then keep it in the forefront of your mind all the time. The calculation is easy of course—divide your yearly salary into 52 weeks, and then each week into however many hours you're employed for. The trickier bit—until you're in the habit—is remembering to check if what you're doing is a valuable use of your time.

Remember that for many organizations, saleries are the largest single chunk of expenses. Even when it's not, it's still a signifi-cant figure. And it's one that you have control over, at least when it comes to you. So you need to ensure that whatever you're doing is a good investment of that bit of your time. If not, you need to be ruthless cutting it out.

RULE 44

You know those people who waste your time? They're also wasting your employers" money, which could be used more effectively by you doing something else. So it's your duty to deal firmly with them (but politely of course).

And you must be just as firm with yourself when you catch yourself procrastinating, filling in time, waiting around, doing pointless stuff, chatting with co-workers, working inefficiently, and so on. Your organization is trusting you to invest their money (that is, your salary) as profitably as possible. Don't let them down.

This is also a useful exercise to go through when your time is pulled in more than one direction. Should you go to this meeting, or get that report finished? Well, which is going to produce the greater return on investment? That should give you your answer.

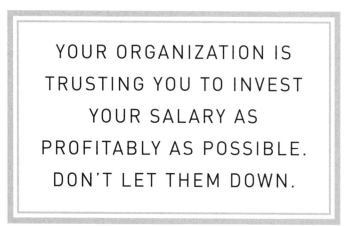

YOUR ORGANIZATION IS TRUSTING YOU TO INVEST YOUR SALARY AS PROFITABLY AS POSSIBLE. DON'T LET THEM DOWN.

RULE 45

Be Proactive, Not Reactive

I know, I know, it takes you all your time just to get the job done, the paperwork handled and the plants watered without having to think about the future or be a brilliant innovator. But the smart manager—that's you again—puts aside 30 minutes a week for forward planning. Try asking yourself simple questions: "How can I generate more sales?" "What can I do more expediently?" "How could I cut staff turnover?" "How can I convert more leads to sales?" "How could I streamline the accounting procedure?" "How could I move into another sector?" "How could I get my team to work harder, faster, brighter?" "How could I get them to brainstorm more freely?" "How could I hold meetings that wouldn't waste so much time?"

There is an old saying, "If you always do what you've always done, you'll always get what you've always gotten." And it's true. If you aren't proactive you'll stagnate. And if you do that the crocodiles will bite your butt. You have to keep paddling, keep moving forward in the water. Sharks have to keep moving forward all their lives to keep water passing through or over their gills. They never stop. Be a shark. Keep moving forward. Because if you don't there will be plenty of others willing to do so.

And believe me I know what it's like. You open your mail box and there are loads of emails to deal with. Then there's the snail mail. Then there's the staff issues. Then there's lunch. Then there's the afternoon work to be done and then there's a panic to get all the mail ready to go out and then there's a quick cup of coffee and then it's about time to pack it all in and go home and there's this idiot telling me I've got to take 30 minutes out of a jam-packed day to think about the future. Yeah, in your dreams.

But that 30 minutes can be combined with another task. Once a week I have lunch on my own and spend the time being proactive, thinking about the future, thinking of ways to be one jump ahead of the competition. But I do have to go out alone for that lunch, or people come and interrupt my mental planning session.

BE A SHARK.
KEEP MOVING
FORWARD.

RULE 46

Be Consistent

If you were to wear a smart business suit every day and then suddenly, without warning, turn up in denim and a worn T-shirt, chances are people would look at you askance.*

If you turn in good work and then one day hand in a pile of junk, people are going to think you've blown it.

If you treat the staff courteously until one day you blow your top and shout at everyone, they won't trust you any more.

If you usually get in early and then one day stroll in around noon smelling of beer, they will stop taking you seriously and accuse you of being a drunk.

People need to know what to expect from you. You have to be consistent. You have to treat all staff the same. Do your work the same. You must avoid drawing the spotlight of gossip down on you. You must be blameless, above reproach (that's probably the same thing), honest, reliable, and dependable. (Again that's probably the same thing.)

* Try it; it's fun. If you don't know what askance is, look it up and then try it.

But you don't have to be gray or dull or boring. You can be exciting, dynamic, stylish, adventurous, innovative, challenging—just make sure that whatever it is you decide to be, you stick at it and be consistent consistently.

IF YOU TURN IN GOOD
WORK AND THEN ONE DAY
HAND IN A PILE OF JUNK,
PEOPLE ARE GOING TO
THINK YOU'VE BLOWN IT.

RULE 47

Set Realistic Targets for Yourself— No, Really Realistic

We're not talking budgets here or corporate targets. We're talking personal goals, personal objectives, personal bottom lines. You have to set them or you won't be able to determine whether you are a success. There's no point, by the way, in judging yourself against anyone else. I always wanted to be terribly good at a sport, but I can't run and failed miserably. It has always led me to believe I am a failure, but I found out the other day that there is a gene for good sporting skills, and it is one I obviously don't have. Am I a failure? Nope, just genetically challenged, and I can't beat myself up about that. I am good at other things and I measure my success against

- How I was doing last year
- How I was doing five years ago
- How I'm doing against my personal targets
- How I'm doing against my long-term plan

There isn't another person in sight because measuring yourself against anyone else is a mug's game.

I once owned a motorcycle—a rather grand one and I loved it very much. I came alongside another motorcyclist at the traffic lights and looked his bike over. "That's the one I want," I cried to myself in the splendid isolation of my crash helmet. He was looking at my bike and obviously thinking the same thing. As the lights changed and we both roared away together, I realized he and I were riding identical bikes. Ah, the fickle mind, how it winds us up, beats us up, and plays tricks. Look at anyone and chances are there will be something to envy, but you don't know what goes on inside them. Walk a mile in someone else's shoes, they say, and chances are you'll be a mile away; but you've got their shoes; make a run for it.

So set yourself some targets but be realistic about them. I'm going to be Emperor of the World may sound impressive but it is totally unrealistic.

Make your targets challenging but attainable, realistic but a bit of a struggle—no good making them too easy, nor too hard.

AH, THE FICKLE MIND,
HOW IT WINDS US UP,
BEATS US UP, AND PLAYS
TRICKS.

Have a Game Plan, but Keep It Secret

No one knows what goes on inside your head. No one knows what lofty heights you aspire to. No one knows what you're really up to—remember Rule 43: Know what you are actually doing—so you can work on your game plan and be doing your job well at the same time. Your game plan should incorporate both long- and short-term goals—where you want to be, where you intend being—and then you have something to match your success against—where you actually are.

Why keep it secret? Because the game plan of your corporation, your management team, and your boss may not exactly match your own game plan. This is a personal game plan and should be kept to yourself to protect your dreams and hopes and aspirations—there is nothing quite like having someone dampen your fireworks. An awful lot of management is about appearances—being able to look the part, to inspire confidence, to walk your walk. If people get wind of any game plan that deviates from that confident air of the perfect manager, they will lose confidence. You might be thinking of striking out on your own, but don't tell anyone or they will assume you are leaving any minute now, even if your plans don't allow for that for several years. If you have a game plan of rapid promotion, people will assume you are an overachiever and stop giving you long-term projects on the grounds that you'll be moving up too soon. And so on. Play your cards close to your chest and keep up the appearance of dedication, commitment, reliability, diligence, and stability—even if in your heart of hearts you are planning a revolution, climbing Everest, or taking over the empire.

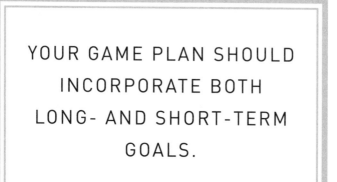

YOUR GAME PLAN SHOULD INCORPORATE BOTH LONG- AND SHORT-TERM GOALS.

RULE 49

Get Rid of Superfluous Rules

Ha, I can hear you thinking, "He's shot himself in the foot now. Get rid of superfluous rules, ha, in a book of rules?" Yep, get rid of superfluous rules. Not my rules of course, not your rules of course. Their rules, obviously. Let people on your team know that you are on their side and will streamline any procedures to enhance efficiency. That means old baggage has to go.

In any workplace there will be a mountain of red tape, bureaucracy, old rules left in place from previous management regimes—get rid of them all. Question everything you and your team do and make it work slicker and quicker by getting rid of anything that is redundant, unnecessary, left over. This is the work equivalent of clutter clearing; practice feng shui if you like.

It's terribly easy to settle into a routine and to stop seeing things with a clear eye, a fresh vision. Every day you have to go into work and see it as an outside consultant would. Question "Why do we do this? Why do we do it like this?" I bet you'll find a lot of clutter and can eliminate it.

I once worked for a company where every letter going out had to be "vetted" by a senior office secretary. She was a bit of a dragon to say the least, and if you ever got on the wrong side of her, your letters went straight to the bottom of the pile—and stayed there. Why did letters have to be routed through her? Beats me, but I had to work unbelievably hard to get rid of that bit of Dickensian nonsense.

Streamline. Save time. Make your people happier and more trusted. Simple really.

WHY DO WE DO THIS?
WHY DO WE DO IT
LIKE THIS?

Learn from Your Mistakes

We all make mistakes—we wouldn't be the wonderfully creative, innovative managers we are if we didn't. But some managers gloss over any mistakes they make. They cover them, bury them, forget about them.

You, as a brilliant manager, won't do that. You won't beat yourself up over them, nor sit in a pit of misery over them but you will analyze what went wrong, discuss with colleagues why it went wrong, and make a plan to prevent it from going wrong again.

Our mistakes could be anything from a badly handled appraisal, a lost sale, a badly thought out report, a poor use of time or resources, a failure to meet a deadline—when you start to write down how many failures there could be, the list is endless.

After you have made your mistake, the important thing to do as well as all the above is to find out the right way to do it next time.

Being a manager is an ongoing learning experience. You never stand still and you never think you know it all—you don't and can't. But you can have trusted people to ask and good reference books at hand to guide you—especially if they are short, sharp, snappy, and practical.*

---

* See, for example, Ros Jay, *Fast Thinking Manager's Manual*, Pearson Education, 2nd edition, 2004.

Mistakes are brilliant because they not only teach us where we went wrong but also how to fix it. You are a better manager, more experienced, have a wider spectrum to call on when you've made a few errors. We all make mistakes—admit them, learn from them, and move on.

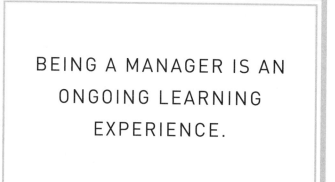

BEING A MANAGER IS AN ONGOING LEARNING EXPERIENCE.

Be Ready to Unlearn—What Works, Changes

You know how it is, you're sailing along doing what you've always done and suddenly you're not making your figures, sales are dropping, staff turnover is going up, things are falling apart. But you're not doing anything you haven't done in the past. You had a winning formula and suddenly it doesn't work any more. What can you do? Well, for a start realize that what works, changes. And it can change so rapidly you didn't realize it until it's too late. Be aware of this; be ready and prepared to adapt quickly. You have to stay abreast of

- Latest innovations in your industry
- New technology
- New terminology
- New methodology
- Changes in sales, market trends, staff turnover figures, targets, and budgets

Don't get stuck in any ruts. Be ready to spin on a dime if you have to. Good management is about adapting to change rapidly and skillfully. If you don't, you go the way of the dinosaurs.

The same goes for all sorts of things—style of management with staff, for instance. You might have a way with them that has worked for years and all of a sudden it doesn't. You could persevere, but you might lose staff rapidly. Better to be ready to unlearn your old ways and adopt new ones. It could be you have changed, unknowingly, unconsciously. If we get stuck in ways of doing things, sometimes we change them without recognizing that change. We have to be alert to those changes that creep in.

GOOD MANAGEMENT IS ABOUT ADAPTING TO CHANGE RAPIDLY AND SKILLFULLY.

RULE 52

Cut the Crap—Prioritize

I used to work for a manager who was fond of asking who we worked for. If we said ourselves, he shook his head. If we said him, he shook his head. If we said the directors, he shook his head. And on and on. The only answer, he said, was the shareholders. And the only reason we worked, he said, was for the profit. Everything else was padding. Fair enough. We do work for the shareholders—whoever they might be. It might be yourself if you are a one-person band. They might be the directors if it's a family-owned firm and not trading on the stock market. They might be millions of little people who have all invested.

So cut the crap. There is only one reason for being in business, no matter what anyone says—profit. To make money. If you're making your figures, good. If you're not, clear your desk out. Simple. Now you have a neat yardstick to judge everything you do. Ask, "Does this contribute toward the profits I am making, or not?" If it does, keep right on doing it. If it doesn't, throw it out.

When all is said and done, that is what it's all about. No money, no business. No business, no job. No job, no mortgage, car, bread on the table, holidays in Tuscany.

I bet if you sit down and look at everything you do, a lot of it will be padding. Time to prioritize. Cut the crap and dedicate yourself to one thing and one thing only—the bottom line. And that's what separates a really sharp manager like you from all the others. That clear focus, that vision, that dedication.

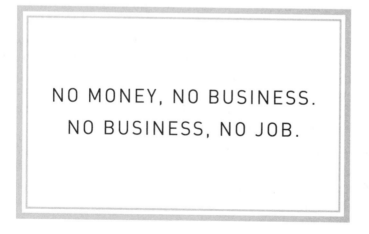

NO MONEY, NO BUSINESS.
NO BUSINESS, NO JOB.

Cultivate Those in the Know

Always remember it's not what you know, but who you know. And in business there are movers and shakers, and there are worker ants. You need to know who the movers and shakers are—and cultivate them. Often senior management have assistants that act as guards—you don't get to talk to God but you do get to be brushed off by God's right-hand assistant. You have to get on the right side of the assistant and that means charm and politeness, tact and discretion, gamesmanship and ruthless cunning.

I once worked for a boss who used a business consultant as his sort of unofficial assistant—she shielded and protected him from having to talk to his staff. Her surname was Burton and everyone called her Mrs. Burton except those in the boss's inner circle who called her JB.

I started to call her JB also and the first few times she looked at me quite horrified—I was only a junior manager and not entitled to do so. But I got away with it. After a few weeks the boss heard me call her JB and assumed I had been accepted into her inner circle of close chums and colleagues. He started to give me more responsibility, which meant she started to give me respect as I was obviously one of his favorites—and they bounced off each other, each believing me to be the other's accepted one and I got preferential treatment from both.

Lots of people think that a) the "old school tie" system is dead; b) if it ain't dead it ought to be; c) it is dead and therefore a new system has taken its place and having to know those in the know no longer counts; and/or d) raw talent will always shine through.

RULE 53

Some of the above may be true. The old school tie thing will never be dead because those in the know are the ones who still run that particular club. It might not be school any more, instead it might be the golf club, charity work, breakfast clubs, university, family, previous places of work, old friends, whatever. People in the know like to collect around them people they also know and therefore can trust. You have to get to know those around those who need to be known: cultivate them and then become one of those around those in the know—and then become one of those in the know. What you do then is entirely up to you.

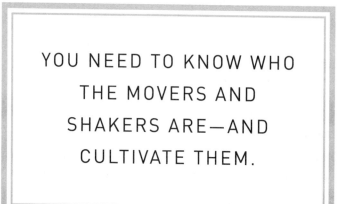

YOU NEED TO KNOW WHO
THE MOVERS AND
SHAKERS ARE—AND
CULTIVATE THEM.

RULE 54

Know When to Kick the Door Shut

Keeping an open-door policy as a manager is a basically good idea, but there comes a time when you have to know it is time to kick the door shut so that you can

- Get some work done.
- Have a meeting in private.
- Let your team know you don't want to be disturbed.
- Let the team know you really are the boss and not really one of them at all.

Obviously a good manager such as yourself likes to have an open-door policy so that the staff have access to you when and as they need. But there are times when it is necessary physically and psychologically to create a barrier. You see, the real secret of good management is that no matter how chummy you are with the team there comes a time when it is essential that you are actually the boss.

Ruling by democracy is all very well; meetings and committees are fine; and joint discussions are rewarding. But when push comes to shove, you have to be prepared to take charge and that means you have to fly by the seat of your pants, make the tough calls, and be the boss. And occasionally shutting the door reinforces that. You don't have to be a cruel or harsh or dictatorial boss, but a boss you must be.

If you are one of those managers who finds it hard to be assertive or "bossy," I suggest you practice kicking the door shut. It is a deeply symbolic gesture about who controls your environment—you. Do it a few times and the team will get the message. After you're used to it, you can control who sits down in your office and how long they stay. It is essential for employees to take you seriously, for you to stamp your authority on the situation. Kicking the door shut symbolizes you are the manager—and this is a good thing, believe me. Oh, and it'll also mean you get some work done without interruption. Just don't do it too often—nothing is more frustrating than a boss who is never available.

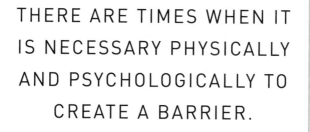

THERE ARE TIMES WHEN IT IS NECESSARY PHYSICALLY AND PSYCHOLOGICALLY TO CREATE A BARRIER.

RULE 55

Fill Your Time Productively and Profitably

After you learn to kick the door shut, you'll find yourself alone in an empty office. But to be the really great and effective manager you are, and are going to be, you don't coast or cruise. You get your head down and get the work done. And you get it done fast and effectively and efficiently. Then you do some work on your long-term goals, your game plan, and your business education. (Don't stand still—read something.)

Working hard when you're not being encouraged with an electric cattle prod is a bit like working for yourself. You have to be motivated, dedicated, and focused. It takes practice and training. We all like to goof off. And that's fine every now and then. We all need thinking time, down time. It is important though not to overdo it.

Don't let the time bandits come in and steal a whole day. Set little deadlines. Make short lists, so you can cross off lots and feel good about what you've done. Get loads of fresh air, or you'll sleep too much. Don't drink alcohol at lunchtime, or you'll sleep afternoons. Go to bed early enough, or you'll be trying to catch up on sleep in the office.

Beware of time-wasting people. Practice telling people you've got something important and urgent to finish and can you come and see them later?

Beware of emails, too—they have a way of sucking time. And they tend to make you terribly reactive—"Oh, I've got a clear in-box; all my work is done." But the truth is, work isn't replying to emails or composing emails—it is getting your sleeves rolled up and actually doing something; making phone calls, chasing people, creating sales, checking production, filing reports. Get on with it, now. Be productive. Be profitable. Everything else can take a hike.

DON'T STAND STILL—
READ SOMETHING.

RULE 56

Have a Plan B and a Plan C

You have to plan for disasters. You've got to build a "what if" clause into everything you do. If you don't, you'll be caught looking inept. Never assume it's all going right—it isn't. Never assume you'll always do OK—you won't. Never assume technology will always work—it won't. Never assume you've got enough time—you haven't. Never assume they'll turn up on time—they won't. Never assume you won't forget things—you will. Never assume Plan A will work—it won't. Never assume Plan B will also work—one day that won't either.

I think you might get the picture by now. When things go wrong—and they will—be ready to improvise, adapt, and overcome. Say you're giving a presentation and have mapped out the whole thing using PowerPoint; what will you do if there is a power outage? Technology failure? You must have worked out beforehand what to do when power fails or technology screws up or that order fails to come in—because they will. Maybe not today, but tomorrow lies waiting to catch you unaware, unguarded, unprepared.

Really good managers, of course, don't need Plan B or Plan C because they can think on their feet and are ready to cover their tracks at any time, ready to improvise. I think it wiser though constantly to ask, "How am I going to cope when this doesn't work?" Serves me every time.

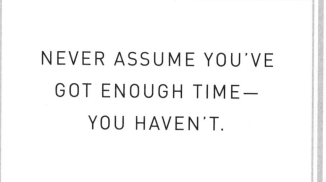

NEVER ASSUME YOU'VE
GOT ENOUGH TIME—
YOU HAVEN'T.

Capitalize on Chance—Be Lucky, but Never Admit It

If you keep your eyes open and your wits about you, there will be opportunities, chances, and bits of random luck. If you are quick and clever and enterprising you can catch the coattails of such moments and ride on the back of them. Such is luck. Grab it while you can because it is a fleeting thing. You can't build it into a plan or a budget or a report, but it will happen all around you. In fact, the more you cherish it and nurture it and look for it, the more it will happen. We have to believe in luck or otherwise how could we attribute the success of people we don't like?

Now don't go building your career on luck; it doesn't work like that. I'm saying we all get a bit lucky from time to time, and when that happens, you have to hang in there and go with it—and then keep quiet about it. You don't always have to tell the truth—and all that false modesty sucks. If you were lucky, say, "It was a lucky break," but say it in such a way that people know months of careful planning went into it, years of research, decades of experience—because that, frankly, is the truth.

There is no such thing as luck alone, but there are random-seeming moments of opportunity which you can grasp because of all that work, experience, research, and planning. If you fail to grasp, the moment will fly past and you'll be none the better for it. But learn to recognize and capitalize on the opportunity, and you can hitch a ride on it. It's all up to you. If you weren't so good at your job, the luck wouldn't happen. If you weren't such a good manager, you wouldn't be quick enough to seize those moments and utilize them.

As U.S. President Thomas Jefferson said, "I am a great believer in luck, and I find the harder I work the more I have of it."

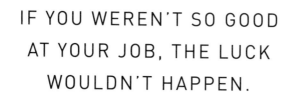

IF YOU WEREN'T SO GOOD
AT YOUR JOB, THE LUCK
WOULDN'T HAPPEN.

RULE 58

Recognize When You're Stressed

The good manager stays well ahead of the stress game. And why? Because stress is counterproductive—it isn't profitable. The old image of the stressed executive popping pills, with high blood pressure but still pulling off fantastic deals is just that—old. The modern executive is laid back, unhurried, charming, thoughtful, careful, on top of their job. You don't need stress. You really, really don't. Yes, you need excitement, challenge, enthusiasm, exhilaration, and stimulation, but you do not need stress.

Stress is just excitement and fun that has gone wrong. Instead of loving your job, you start to fear it. Instead of being excited, you experience fear. Instead of challenge, it's confrontation.

So how do you manifest stress? No really, how do you experience it? This is such a personal thing. I know when I'm under a lot of stress because I shout more, reason less, demand more, am polite less, rush more, and am laid back less. But that's me. For you it might be smoking or drinking more or not sleeping or not eating (or eating too much or too hurriedly or too much junk food) or it might show as nervous exhaustion (sleeping too much), panic attacks, twitches, tics, irrational fears, inappropriate behavior, driving too fast (me again as well to that one). If you don't know what your signs are, ask somebody who knows you well—they will be able to tell you.

When I notice a couple of my stress symptoms, I take time out to check

- Why am I stressed?
- What is causing the stress?
- What can I do about it?
- How can I stop it recurring again?

I don't like being stressed (my children say I am a real pain) and there is no job worth doing that I'm going to allow to affect my health detrimentally. I know how to chill—I'm very good at lowering the stress levels once I notice they've crept up. I know what works for me. What works for you?

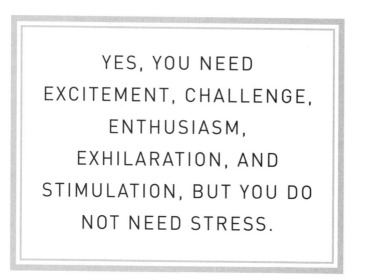

YES, YOU NEED EXCITEMENT, CHALLENGE, ENTHUSIASM, EXHILARATION, AND STIMULATION, BUT YOU DO NOT NEED STRESS.

Manage Your Health

It's easy to put off managing your health. Do it now. The general advice is

- Eat properly—sitting down in a relaxed setting, taking time to enjoy your food.
- Eat proper food—fresh, organic, lean meat, fresh fruit, salads, vegetables, roughage, no junk, no processed food.
- Get a decent night's sleep—every night.
- Stop worrying—laugh, have fun, enjoy something not work-related.
- Carry out basic health checks regularly to catch major conditions in time, such as testicular or breast lumps and bumps.
- Work in a comfortable and safe environment.
- Get yourself screened from time to time for cholesterol levels, blood pressure, and so on.
- Have supportive and loving relationships.
- Have some sort of belief system to sustain you in times of crisis.
- Exercise.
- Watch your weight.
- Drink moderately.
- Don't smoke.*

* Of all of them, this is the biggie apparently and will do more than all the others put together to contribute to your overall life expectancy and health.

Of course you don't have to do any of this. You're a grown-up and can make your own decisions. But if you want to live long and prosper, it pays to think now.

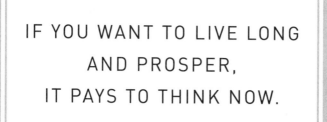

IF YOU WANT TO LIVE LONG
AND PROSPER,
IT PAYS TO THINK NOW.

RULE 60

Be Prepared for the Pain and Pleasure

Look, working for a living is always going to be a mixed bag. And the higher up you go, the more true this is. As a lowly accounts clerk, back when I first started out, I got used to being bored, idle, irritated, frustrated, and sick of the job. By the time I had risen to being a general manager, I was strangely surprised to find myself also bored, idle, irritated, frustrated, and sick of the job.

But whereas when I was starting out I didn't expect any different, by the time I had risen to the heights I was totally unprepared for the same feelings. I guess I expected every day to be dramatic, exciting, utterly challenging, demanding, and knife-edge stuff. And when it wasn't, I was, I guess, disappointed.

Now, of course, I realize that not every day can be fantastic. Some days will be boring. Some days will be adrenaline-filled and dramatic—but not as many as will be boring. You have to be prepared for the pain and the pleasure. You have to adjust your expectations so that you don't get irritated when it is boring, and don't explode with pleasure when it is too exciting for words.

Trouble is, if it is boring, you might be tempted, as indeed I have been on many occasions, to liven it up a bit by being disruptive. Best sit on your hands and let the feeling pass. As a manager you aren't allowed to be disruptive—except in an innovative way of course.

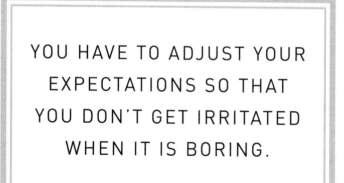

YOU HAVE TO ADJUST YOUR
EXPECTATIONS SO THAT
YOU DON'T GET IRRITATED
WHEN IT IS BORING.

Face the Future

Whatever you are doing now, things are going to change. It is inevitable that the future will soon be upon us. Things will change; they have to. People you now work with will leave your team. Your sales figures will improve/slacken off. Your boss will retire/move on. Your customers will change. Your colleagues will be different. You, too, will change.

All these changes happen, and it is the smart manager who not only embraces them but is also prepared for them. Earlier we looked at having a Plan B and a Plan C; well, this is different—this is not catering for a specific crisis but being fluid and flexible enough to stay ahead of the game. What this means is that when change occurs you can take it in your stride and aren't thrown off course by it.

I once worked for a particular company that got taken over twice, in the space of a year. Each time the new people came in, they had a whole series of changes to implement. They wanted things done "their way." This was fine, but after the first time we had barely got our breath back when the second takeover occurred.

I watched a lot of people fall by the wayside because they couldn't cope with the stress of having to stay so flexible. I was nearly one of them myself. It was a hard time but I saw then that resisting change was futile. Only by embracing the change could I survive—and not only survive but also milk the situation to my advantage. The more I smiled and had a sort of "bring it on attitude" the more responsibility I was given for the change itself. Other man-agers played the oak in the storm, but I was the willow. I bent and swayed and survived. They resisted, stood firm, and lost branches.

You have to face your own future as well. Will you move on? Have you grown bored with the job, the industry, your role in it? What turns you on today may not in 10 years' time.

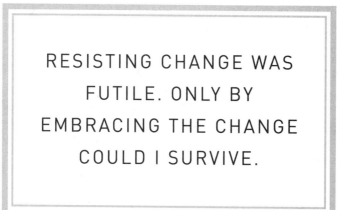

RESISTING CHANGE WAS FUTILE. ONLY BY EMBRACING THE CHANGE COULD I SURVIVE.

RULE 62

Head Up, Not Head Down

It's easy to adopt a head-down approach to life. It's harder to remain cheerful; head up. Is your glass half empty or half full? If it seems to be half empty, perhaps you need a holiday, a retraining schedule, a few new challenges, a new job, a new department, a new team—or simply a new approach. Life does tend to get fired at us at point-blank range and there is barely time to duck. The manager's lot is not always a happy or easy one and you get tired, despondent, bored, listless, and just about ready to quit. We all do from time to time. Being a manager can feel like a thankless task. You get stuff shoveled at you from all directions. I'm never sure whether it's better to be at the top shoveling stuff downward or at the bottom shoveling stuff upward but I sure as hell know it's not great caught in the middle fending it off from above and below.

Head up is both an affirmation (repeat it to yourself constantly when encountering problems, but silently, only to yourself, or they will devour you) and a physical instruction—you can physically and emotionally (and probably mentally) practice head up.

While looking in a mirror, keep your head up and say, "I feel really miserable." You will laugh. Try the opposite. Head down, and say, "I feel really happy." Again you will find it impossible and silly. You will laugh. But you have to be looking in a mirror. Perhaps you always look like that. Either way it is funny. You are funny.

When entering a room, it is head up. When chairing a meeting, it is head up. When doing a presentation, it is head up. When greeting people, it is head up. When talking to staff, it is head up. When talking to customers, it is head up. At the end of a long and busy day, when you go to bed, you can do head down—and go to sleep knowing you've been big and bright and bold all day. Well done you.

PHYSICALLY AND
EMOTIONALLY (AND
PROBABLY MENTALLY)
PRACTICE HEAD UP.

RULE 63

See the Forest *and* the Trees

You've got to see the big picture. It's no good concentrating solely on what you do or what your department does. You can't even keep your gaze limited to what your organization does, or even what your industry does. You've got to see the wider view all the time. The good manager—that's you*— needs to have a good grasp of politics—both national and world—social history, world events, national intentions, international concerns, the environment, current legislation, proposed legislation** and technological developments (ones that may or may not affect your industry).

But you've also got to keep a close watch on what is going on under your nose—your team, your department, your immediate surroundings, the fine details as well as the big picture.

And how are you going to find the time to think about these things? To reflect, to analyze, to anticipate? You're going to schedule it on your calender, that's how. That's what proper grown-up managers do. And if you want to be a talented senior manager, you need to recognize the importance of giving yourself space to think. Sometimes you get the opportunity when you're traveling. (But make sure you deliberately

---

* I keep saying, "That's you." You may wonder how I know. Because you are reading this. Bad managers think they know it all. You are prepared to read, to learn, to seek the advice of others, to widen your horizons, to have opinions, to stay abreast of current and new ideas and to keep an open mind by reading this far. That's good. You are good. Well done you.

** No, not just legislation that affects your industry but all big proposed legislation. You'd be surprised how often the "domino" effect affects you.

allocate the time, and use it wisely.) Sometimes you have to block out an hour or two in your calendar and make sure you're not disturbed. Call it "planning time" if anyone asks—unless they're a successful manager themselves, in which case they'll understand.

The bright manager has to keep their eyes and ears open, their wits about them, their mind open to new ideas and innovations and trends. You've got to see the trees *and* the forest.

> IT'S NO GOOD
> CONCENTRATING SOLELY
> ON WHAT YOU DO OR WHAT
> YOUR DEPARTMENT DOES.

RULE 64

Know When to Let Go

Sometimes it's really hard to let go, to know when to stop. But some projects just aren't going to work. Some team members are never going to fit in. Some bosses are never going to be possible to work with. Some situations must simply cease.

The good manager knows instinctively when to back off, to bail out, to retreat, to walk away whistling, pride intact and dignity in place. This rule is for you but also for all the people who get caught, fool around, play up, try to defend the indefensible. Come on, know when to quit, know when the dog is dead.

A good manager knows when to hold his hands up, "Yep, I messed up. It was my fault. I surrender." Invariably you'll be forgiven because such an honest, direct approach throws 'em off the trail and they don't know how to handle you.

If you don't know when to let go, you'll build up anger, resentment, stress, jealousy, and pain. Learn to shrug and walk. You don't have to forgive or forget or anything, except drop it and walk away.

RULE 64

There is a myth in business that to get even is better than getting mad. But getting even is getting mad; it just takes a bit longer. Let it go. Concentrate on the next big exciting thing you can do.

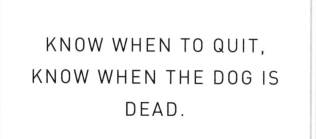

KNOW WHEN TO QUIT, KNOW WHEN THE DOG IS DEAD.

Be Decisive, Even if It Means Being Wrong Sometimes

I bet you hate the type of manager who refuses to make a decent decision in case they make the wrong one. The indecisive, frightened manager who won't decide until it's too late or they get the decision made for them. I've worked for a few and there is nothing more irritating than someone who fence-sits because they don't know which way to jump—and all in the name of fear. They are frightened to decide in case they make a mistake—one that might cost them their job. Big deal. Better to jump and make a mistake than to sit there too frightened to make a move. Bring it on.

And suppose it does turn out to be the wrong decision. Well, sometimes out of big mistakes something bright and shiny and magical appears, and we land on our feet with a tra-la and manage to look good despite sometimes not knowing what we were doing. This is the magic manager that I want you to be. The instinctive manager around whom anything can happen—and will. If you want to sit on a fence, go find another book to read.

Now I'm not saying here that you should make rash, ill-thought-through decisions. I'm assuming as a good manager that if it's that kind of decision, you have looked at the evidence before you and evaluated it, maybe asked for views from others. It's that point in the process I'm talking about—the point where you are tempted to shy away from the decision, in case it turns out to be the wrong one.

This is about courage. The courage to be wrong sometimes. The courage to take a risk. The courage to be scared in a good way. (Sitting on a fence because you are scared is a lot different from taking a big decision and being scared but exhilarated.)

All you have to do is look at the facts, evaluate them, ask advice, listen to your intuition and then do it—make the decision. Be dynamic, be bold.

> BETTER TO JUMP AND
> MAKE A MISTAKE THAN TO
> SIT THERE TOO
> FRIGHTENED TO MAKE A
> MOVE.

RULE 66

Adopt Minimalism as a Management Style

Minimalism means not issuing lengthy reports. It means not issuing memos every 20 minutes. It means keeping rules to the minimum* and letting people get on with their jobs. It means mission statements that make sense, are clear and easy to understand and are simple. It means management where managers use professionals and let them get on with their tasks in peace and quiet. It means managers who are secure in themselves and don't need to score points, bully, or interfere.

Minimalist management is all about getting more by doing less. Yes, sure you have to be the boss, but it's more like steering a big ship—the tiniest touch of the wheel is enough. You swing that wheel violently from side to side and you're off course in an instant.

---

* No, not these Rules, I mean the petty ones—you have to wear a tie, you have to have one doughnut, not two at coffee time, you have to address senior management as Mr./Mrs. X and not use their first names, you have to park within the lines, you have to wear sensible shoes, you have to…you know what I mean.

RULE 66

There is an old Chinese saying: "Govern a country the same way you cook small fish," that is, don't keep fiddling with them or they fall apart. Manage a department, team, or company in pretty much the same way—gently, discreetly, unobtrusively. Better to be understated than too obvious.

MINIMALIST MANAGEMENT
IS ALL ABOUT GETTING
MORE BY DOING LESS.

RULE 67

Visualize Your Plaque

When you write your bestseller and then die you will get a plaque on the building where you were born, or lived, or wrote the damn thing—just so long as it was in London.* When I say "you" I don't mean you, I mean whoever it is that lives there after you've croaked. This plaque is there to commemorate the fact that you did a good thing while you were alive. If you didn't do your good thing—that is, write your bestseller, add to the sum of human literacy, manage to afford to live in London—you don't get a plaque.

Now imagine that there is a plaque for management style and it's not limited to London. What would you get yours for? Would you in fact get one? Basically, how would you like to be remembered? I worked for a boss once whose style of management was quaint to say the least. As he came in each day he would blast the first person he saw, give them a complete thrashing for whatever they happened to be doing. Then he would go to his office and have coffee for half an hour. Then he would walk through the plant and compliment the first person he saw, tell them what a great job they were doing no matter what it was they were doing. I asked him about this and he said, "Keeps them on their toes. They never know where they are with me. I get more out of them if they are frightened." No plaque for you, Billy boy.

---

* I'm fairly certain you have to be dead, but you don't have to have written anything. Being a musician is good enough—even Jimi Hendrix got one.

I've told this before because it still, after more than 20 years, fascinates me as the worst incompetent, bullying stupidity I have ever come across. And he is still in a job, still employed by the same firm. Yes, he has hardly risen up the ranks because he is still doing pretty much what he was then, back when I knew him, but he is still employed. I don't buy shares in that particular company—never have, never will.

I want a plaque. I want it for being the best damn manager there ever was. I want it for being good for my team, getting results, setting standards; for being a huge success and somebody they liked working for.

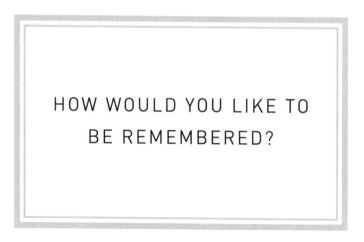

HOW WOULD YOU LIKE TO BE REMEMBERED?

RULE 68

Have Principles and Stick to Them

When you think about it, you've got to have principles. If you don't, you end up despising yourself or in debt or in prison. You might end up like this anyway, but at least you could say, "But I have my principles."

There has to be a line beyond which you will not go. You have to know where that line is drawn. No one else has to know until they ask you to cross it, and then you can tell them. That line has to be a 10-mile-high solid steel wall. You can't go beyond it, no matter what.

I have a friend whose boss once asked her to falsify a formal warning letter to present at a meeting for a member of staff who had been fired and was claiming unfair dismissal. Would you do this? Does it matter whether you think the person was rightly or wrongly dismissed? Suppose they had been warned but it hadn't been recorded in writing? Suppose you and your boss were sure it must have been put in writing at the time, but you can't find it now? I'm not telling you what's right or wrong in this instance. I'm saying that you have to know what you consider to be right or wrong. And then stand by it.

So where would you draw your line? I've been asked to do things I didn't like. I've been asked to do things I found unpleasant. I've been asked to do things I found extremely irksome, but whenever I've been asked to cross my own personal line—which thankfully in a long business career has been only once or twice—I was able to say, "No," and stick to it. And each time I got a pat on the back rather than a trip to the HR office.

> THERE HAS TO BE A LINE
> BEYOND WHICH YOU WILL
> NOT GO. YOU HAVE TO
> KNOW WHERE THAT LINE
> IS DRAWN.

RULE 69

Follow Your Intuition

Deep down inside you know when you're right, and you know when you're wrong. Sure we can cut off that inner voice, but if we do we lose touch, and then we really are in trouble. That inner intuition may not speak loud and clear all the time but when it does, you'd be mad not to follow it.

Trouble is your mind also speaks loud and clear—all the time—and we mix the two up and follow what we think is intuition when in fact it is fear or jealousy or another emotion.

So how do you tell? If when you're talking to somebody about a new system you are about to implement and, though they look positive, you feel an odd or cold feeling inside, listen to it. Take time to think why. Tell somebody else about it and see if it happens again. Go back to the plan and look at it from all viewpoints, considering all the stakeholders. Are you still convinced?

Never be too proud or too lazy to get more feedback, to find a sounding board or to rethink a proposal or a decision if you've got a bad feeling about it.

Look at previous good or bad decisions you've made. How did you feel about them at the time? Did you, deep down, know a bad course of action was flawed before you followed it? Would you know that feeling again?

Developing your intuition is a hard thing to teach, but if you make a habit of "listening" to how you feel about something, your radar will improve, and you'll begin to know when a gut feeling is telling you that something isn't right.

IF YOU MAKE A HABIT OF "LISTENING" TO HOW YOU FEEL ABOUT SOMETHING, YOUR RADAR WILL IMPROVE.

RULE 70

Be Creative

The good manager keeps a virtual closet full of creative techniques so that when she gets stuck, when the team gets stuck—and you and the team will from time to time—you have something to fall back on.

Being creative is about finding new and different ways to solve problems. You get stuck and start worrying and then you go off and tend your garden, do some washing up, fly a kite or whatever, and you get immersed in what you are doing and answers bubble up to the surface.

Most creative techniques get you to switch off your conscious, thinking brain and start to use a deeper, more intuitive part of your mind. And that part has a whole load of answers that we can't normally access. This is the part we can access during sleep or meditation or by using creative thinking techniques.

Watch what other managers do—the ones you admire and respect. They probably have a virtual closet of creative tricks. Borrow a few. Read up on creative thinking techniques. Find out what the bright managers are doing, thinking, trying out. Ask somebody not in your field what they would do. Don't be afraid to be wacky or off the wall—after all some of the best ideas have come from dreams.

GET IMMERSED IN WHAT
YOU ARE DOING AND
ANSWERS BUBBLE UP TO
THE SURFACE.

Don't Stagnate

So are you a leader or a manager? Not really a fair question when we've spent the whole book so far making sure you are an effective, efficient, and startlingly good manager. But the really good managers are also leaders—they inspire and motivate, encourage and enthuse. They draw people to them like moths to a flame. They are charismatic and dynamic and stylish. They are leaders indeed.

But they are also good managers. Too much management and you stagnate. You have to revel in change, seek new challenges, stay on your toes, find new ways of doing things, motivate your team in new and exciting ways, introduce new technology and ideas, start trends, jump fences, light fires. You can't be seen to stand still or moss will grow over you and you become a fixture and people stop noticing you.

I know it's difficult sometimes to see beyond today's workload, tomorrow's meetings, next week's directors" report. But you have to be moving or you will stagnate. Set aside a little time each day or week—only half an hour perhaps—to think up new ways of being revolutionary. Why? Because if you don't do this you become bogged down in the day-to-day, the humdrum, the routine. Yes, you are a manager, but you are also an innovator, motivator, inspirer, leader, and trendsetter.

If the moss has already grown over you and people have come to regard you as part of the furniture, you will have to work very hard to shake off that image. Don't scare them with radical change—do it bit by bit.

> THE REALLY GOOD
> MANAGERS ARE ALSO
> LEADERS—THEY INSPIRE
> AND MOTIVATE,
> ENCOURAGE AND
> ENTHUSE.

RULE 72

Be Flexible and Ready to Move On

There will come a time when it's time to move on. Other jobs are waiting to be done. Other teams are waiting to be led. You may have to pack up camp and hit the trail. So keep your eyes open for opportunities. As Thomas Edison once said, "Opportunity is missed by most people because it comes dressed in overalls and looks like work."

Remember your long-term plan—and I bet it didn't include stuff like, "Stay here until I retire and/or turn to dust"—and keep looking to distant horizons.

Being a good manager, a fantastic manager, often means you get sought out, head-hunted, poached. Be ready to be enticed away. Doesn't mean you have to go, but be open to offers— how flattering.

Stay on your toes and be ready to move laterally; be prepared to look at unusual opportunities. Be ready perhaps to go it alone if that's in your long-term plan.

Should you feel guilty at abandoning your team? No. You have a career and that involves moving on. Your team may benefit from a breath of fresh air coming in after you to blow the cobwebs away. I've left managerial jobs where the staff seemed genuinely surprised that I would dare to leave, to spread my wings and go "elsewhere," as if it were a dark and dangerous country that would gobble me up. Of course, once I had left I gained a reputation as a "deserter" for leaving, but better that than "good riddance."

BE READY TO MOVE LATERALLY; BE PREPARED TO LOOK AT UNUSUAL OPPORTUNITIES.

Remember the Object of the Exercise

My fellow writer Carmel McConnell says in *Get Ahead; Give a Damn*: "Happy, fulfilled, stretched but supported people generally achieve the most at work and get the most from life. They drain a lot of swamps—and have a pretty good time doing it (strange though it may seem swamp drainage is a Very Enjoyable Occupation). However, many of us face a few alligators…those subversive obstacles that get in the way of a productive, high achieving but low-stress kind of life. Some of them we make ourselves, some of them are placed there by other people. Some of them just are."

And the object of the exercise, my friend, is what? We all have a different agenda. You may say, "To make profits for the shareholders" (Rule 52), but you're just trying to curry favor by giving an answer you think I want. I don't.

Remember that even when you are up to your ass in alligators the object of the exercise was to drain the swamp. There are many objectives, many swamp-draining exercises. You might see it as the next project, setting the next budget, getting through the next interview, week or disciplinary interview. It might be long-term stuff, career in general, and so on. And the alligators who bite your ass could be colleagues, customers, clients, bosses, staff, family, you name it/them. But they do get in the way of draining the swamp.

This is a Rule about focusing so that you don't get side-tracked by all the nonsense that goes on around you. Stay focused and keep the objective in your sights at all times—whatever it may be.

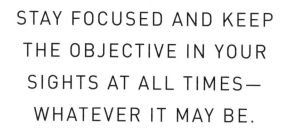

STAY FOCUSED AND KEEP
THE OBJECTIVE IN YOUR
SIGHTS AT ALL TIMES—
WHATEVER IT MAY BE.

Remember That None of Us Has to Be Here

I once worked with a fabulous manager. Sadly he is no longer with us but I remember all the managerial stuff he taught me. He was one of us—seemingly. On the surface he played the company game, discreet, charming, efficient, hard-working, but deep down this man worked for no one but himself.

Bob was an individualist, a rule breaker (but not these Rules—most of these came from him), nonconformist, maverick. He trod a fine line. He was Mr. Cool Dude.

Sure he got the job done and done extremely well, but he was a managerial rebel. He and I were scheduled once to go on a manager's training course. Guess who failed to show up? Yep, Bob. He wasn't going to make LEGO® models for anyone.

I went. I made LEGO® models. I toed the company line. Guess who got promoted? Yep, right again. Bob.

So how did we get here? Ah, moaning. I moaned. Bob would say, "None of us has to be here." And he meant it. Literally. Literally none of us has to be here. We don't have to do the job. We can walk any time we want. This means we are here by choice. We have chosen to be here. We choose to be here each and every day. It is our choice. If we have chosen to be here, then surely it means we are enjoying it—or we wouldn't be here? Right? If we aren't enjoying it, then we should choose not to be here.

Basically what Bob was saying to me was, "Stop moaning—enjoy it or leave." This doesn't mean you can't point out the things that are wrong, but if they aren't going to get solved you'd better learn to live with them. Enjoy it or move over and let someone else do the job who will. None of us has to be here.

STOP MOANING—
ENJOY IT
OR LEAVE.

RULE 75

Go Home

Another manager I worked with stayed late, got in early, skipped lunch, and kept his head down and worked every second he was there. Guess who got promoted over him? Yep, Bob again from Rule 74. Mr. Cool Dude.

One of Bob's favorite lines, to me anyway, was, "Go home, Rich, go home. You've got a young family; go home and see them before they forget what you look like. Either that or send them a photo before they really forget." Naturally I went home. As did Bob, a lot. In fact he was at work so little he got promoted again.

His secret? His team, of which I was one, would have done anything for him. We went that extra mile. We would never have willingly let him down. Bob inspired loyalty in his staff in a way I've rarely seen since. He made all of us feel grown-up, trusted, treated in a respectful way. He never shouted, abused, put upon, demanded, overworked, or humiliated his team. I never saw him have to discipline anyone, ever. He was charismatic and charming, cool and relaxed.

He said his secret was his family. For them he worked. He adored his children and would rather have been home with them than working. His love for them showed, and he wore the badge of a happy family man with great pride. He talked a lot about his kids and his wife and was obviously very happy with them.

He never stayed late because that would have been disloyal to his number-one priority—his family. This gave him great depth. He was well rounded and balanced. He was at ease with himself. He had nothing to prove at work because he was content at home. I've worked with some complete bastards, and I can say the only thing they all had in common was a bad home life. Their base camp was corrupt, and it showed. So, my dear friend, go home.

> HE HAD NOTHING TO PROVE AT WORK BECAUSE HE WAS CONTENT AT HOME.

Keep Learning—Especially from the Opposition

We've all heard the managers who get angry when the competition steals a client from them. Or who rail about how unfair it was that they lost such and such an order. Or when a client leaves, screaming bloody murder that they've been set up. Wrong, wrong, wrong. Believe me, if the competition is stealing your ideas, your customers, your contracts, your clients, your sales, your staff and your income, then you have a) no one to blame but yourself and b) been given a great opportunity to learn how to do it better.

Nothing teaches us better than better competitors. What is it they are doing? What can we learn from this? How can we emulate them? How can we take what they are doing and really run with it? How can we grow our market share by outdoing what they are doing?

Spend some time each week checking what the competition is doing, because if they are effective (and competition invariably is) they will be checking out what you are doing. Spend some time getting to know—and sharing with—the competition. Look, if you have five main competitors and you share with them, you are giving each one a part of what you are doing. But the idea spreads and five will give you ideas, information, research, and so on. We should never fear competition. Embrace it. It grows the market. It keeps you on your toes. It gives you a real learning opportunity—real as in it is actually happening and isn't a training exercise. And it doesn't involve LEGO®.

If you fear competition, what you really fear is your own incompetence. If you know you're doing a good job, the competition can't touch you. If you're not doing a good job, the competition can walk all over you—and you know it, just as you know you're not doing a good job.

> IF YOU FEAR
> COMPETITION,
> WHAT YOU REALLY FEAR
> IS YOUR OWN
> INCOMPETENCE.

RULE 77

Be Passionate and Bold

If you're not going to be passionate about your work, what are you going to be passionate about? Look, you spend more time at work doing work, living, breathing, and being at work, than anything else except perhaps sleeping. You must be passionate about what you do. You're passionate about sex, but that doesn't last as long as your career. You're passionate about food, and you only eat three times a day—work is continual. You're passionate about your life, your hobbies, your family, your holidays. And yet an awful lot of people see their work as something to dread, a chore to be endured. If it's like that for you, then go home—and stay there. Make room for someone who is going to be passionate about it. But I'm positive that isn't you.

When I first started my career—of which I have had several—I read up on the industry before I started training. I read about its history, the famous people in it, stories about it, how it evolved and the legislation surrounding it, and how certain traditions associated with it came about. I went into that job a walking encyclopaedia of facts and information, anecdotes and history. And I had my breath taken away by how little everyone else in that industry knew. I was passionate and it seemed no one else was. I found only a terribly small group of people who cared about what they did. Over the years I have met many others, but never enough.

When you are passionate you can be bold because you have that drive, that enthusiasm, that courage, that excitement. Being bold means you can take risks. And taking risks means they pay off—not all the time but often enough that you get a name for yourself as a high-flyer, a go-getter, a success.

Being passionate means caring about what you do. Not just going through the motions but really caring. Being driven—being constantly excited and enthusiastic. What you do makes a difference—it's not just about the money or the status or the perks. It's about making a real contribution to people's lives and the environment and society. If you're not passionate, what are you? If you are passionate, what are you passionate about? If not now, when?

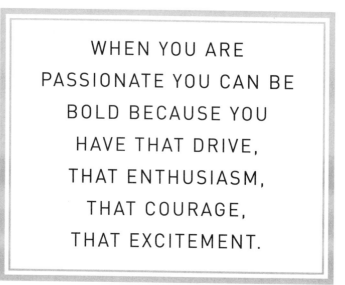

WHEN YOU ARE
PASSIONATE YOU CAN BE
BOLD BECAUSE YOU
HAVE THAT DRIVE,
THAT ENTHUSIASM,
THAT COURAGE,
THAT EXCITEMENT.

RULE 78

Plan for the Worst, but Hope for the Best

As a manager, you should prepare for the worst and hope for the best. What's your worst-case scenario? All the staff phone in sick because it's the NCAA Tournament? You lose that big order? Sales slump to zero? Building burns down? National strikes? Flu epidemic? Terrorist attack? Oil spillage? Health and Safety close you down? All or any of these things can play havoc with your budget figures.

So what contingency plans do you have in place in case this worst-case scenario actually happens? Huh? Yep, thought so. You've got to have emergency plans, panic routes mapped out, procedures for crisis management, actions wrapped up and in the bag, replacement crews sorted, alternative sources of income determined. You have to have a plan.

Now chances are you won't ever have to implement this plan. With luck and divine intervention, it will always remain a plan—nothing more. But a plan you have to have.

RULE 78

Now, you are allowed to hope. Hope it ain't never gonna happen. Hope the sun will forever shine. I was once asked by a special committee what I would do in the event of a major bomb scare at the company where I worked. My answer, "Hope it's a hoax," made them laugh but earned me no brownie points at all. "What about a plan?" I was asked. "Oh, I've got one of those as well," I said, and I may have recovered about half a point. Have a plan—and a lot of hope.

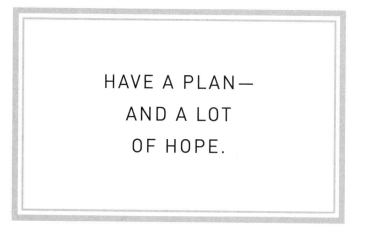

HAVE A PLAN—
AND A LOT
OF HOPE.

Let the Company See You Are on Its Side

To let the company see you are on its side, you need to do some concrete things such as

- Buy some shares.
- Read the company newsletter—better still, edit the damn thing.
- Support company functions.
- Show an interest.
- Ask questions.
- Have your interest in the company noticed and recorded in some way.
- Focus on what you contribute to the company, not on what you get out of it.
- Use the company's products or services.
- Actively speak well of the company.
- Rehearse saying what you think is good about the company—have a ready answer if asked.
- Know the company's mission statement and philosophy.
- Know the company's products and/or services inside and out.
- Know the company history—its formation, its mergers and acquisitions, and such, its long-term goals and its key personnel (founder, and more).
- Know the company's social standing and what it does for the community.

What you do not do—ever—is bad-mouth the company, under any circumstances.

"But, but, but," I hear you say, "Won't this make me out to be a yes-person, a lackey, a company mouthpiece?" Nope. Not if you do it right. If you mouth platitudes and seem insincere, people will know it is an act and that you are a company pawn. But if you are strong about it, people will take your lead and follow suit. Set an example. Be outspoken in your praise for the company. It is such an unfashionable thing to do so you will make your mark, but you do have to be sincere and bold.

"But what if I don't feel so good about the company?" Then get out. It's a two-way process. They employ you. You work for them. You give and they give. You take and they take. If you're unhappy about this relationship, then get out, get a divorce, find another lover. You have to love your company and see it as a relationship. If you're in a bad one, what are you going to do about it? Put up and shut up? I do hope not.

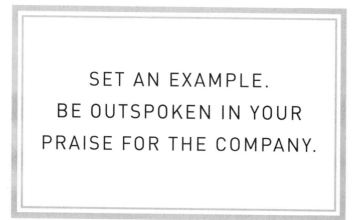

SET AN EXAMPLE.
BE OUTSPOKEN IN YOUR
PRAISE FOR THE COMPANY.

Don't Bad-Mouth Your Boss

OK, so your boss is a jerk and you can't stand working under such a weasel, and you've just got to tell everyone you meet what a fool this boss is. Yes? No. Wrong, wrong, wrong. You do not bad-mouth your boss under any circumstances. OK so your whole team knows your boss is useless and they make that clear to you. Do you agree? No, you do not. Never, ever. If you can't find anything good to say, then say nothing at all. You do not criticize them even if they deserve it, or you feel they do anyway.

Your boss is your boss. If they are that dreadful, then don't work for them, go look someplace else. If you are going to work for them, then that is your choice and you have to stick with it, live with it, support it, believe in it—or you'll go mad.

If your boss is a nightmare, it is your job to turn that around. Get them to trust you. Then get them to delegate to you. Then get them to hand over responsibility to you. Then replace them. Simple, isn't it? Obviously not, but these are the steps you must take if you are serious and committed.

Watch what you say about your boss in case it gets back to his boss—who might just happen to be a fan of your boss and not take kindly to you bad-mouthing them. After all, they put them there and for you to question that decision publicly leaves you in a precarious situation.

I once worked for a complete son of a…who drank, kept bad company, and didn't know if it were New York or the New Year most of the time. Someone complained about him to the head office, and the HR director was sent to take statements. Twelve junior managers, including myself, were questioned about his behavior. I refused to cooperate and said nothing. A year later my boss was still there and I was still there but 11 other junior managers no longer worked for that company. Moral: Keep quiet if you can't be nice. How come he survived? Beats me. He obviously had friends in the right places. How did I survive? No idea. He trusted me and I kept my head down and got on with my job; his behavior didn't affect me unduly and I coped.

> IF YOU CAN'T FIND
> ANYTHING GOOD TO SAY,
> THEN SAY NOTHING
> AT ALL.

Don't Bad-Mouth Your Team

So you can't bad-mouth the company and you can't criticize your boss. "Surely," I hear you ask, "I can criticize my team?" Not in public you can't. Behind closed doors when there is no one there but you and you alone, then and only then are you allowed one small silent scream when things really hit the fan, but apart from that, nothing.

It's a poor work person who blames their tools. Your team is your tool to getting your management job done. If your team is useless it is you who hasn't sharpened the tool, oiled it, cleaned the rust off, repaired the handle, replaced worn out bits, checked for damage, that sort of thing.

Your team will make mistakes; that's a given. Things will go wrong, that too is a given. You're dealing with people; they screw up from time to time, get emotional, let you down, fail to work as a team, goof off, and generally behave completely normally. You'd be a fool not to expect this, to plan for it, to build it into your plans. Look, things go wrong and bad mouthing your team doesn't help. Learn from it and move on.

You have to "publicly celebrate those who move the organization closer to the attainment of its vision and strategic goal"—that's your team, that is. If you criticize your team, you are focusing on the negative, which will spiral them downward. If you praise them it's an uplifting experience.

If you criticize your team, you condemn yourself and are admitting publicly you are a crappy manager. Don't do it—you're not.

THINGS GO WRONG AND
BAD MOUTHING YOUR
TEAM DOESN'T HELP.
LEARN FROM IT AND
MOVE ON.

Accept that Some Things Bosses Tell You to Do Will Be Wrong

Just because you do your job well doesn't mean everyone else does. Some bosses are useless and there's no getting around that. Sometimes they will tell you to do stuff that is crazy. Sometimes they will issue orders that are so obviously off the wall you can't help but gasp. Sometimes they will tell you to do things that are completely wrong. What are you to do?

You have various options:

- Refuse.
- Leave.
- Seek advice from your union/management advisory body/ trade body if you are in one.
- Ask advice from Human Resources.
- Ask advice from other managers.
- Ask advice from your boss's boss.
- Put your concerns in writing.
- Do the work but grumble a lot.
- Do it with a cheerful smile and a whistle.
- Talk to your boss about your misgivings.

Initially it might be polite to go and talk to your boss in person, face-to-face, over an informal coffee; a chat, nothing too heavy. Point out you think you have a problem with their order. Don't make it personal. Don't attack them. Don't tell them they are crap. Explain that it is you that has the problem. The order and your boss are fine but you feel uncomfortable. Put the ball firmly back in their lap. If they insist, end by saying you still feel uncomfortable about it and would like time to seek further advice. Ask if you can put your fears in writing and whether they would do the same.

Sometimes you have to accept that bosses don't know what they are doing, ain't going to change, and you have to put up with it. Or you could simply refuse or leave. Your call. The Rule is that you should accept it happens from time to time.

> SOMETIMES YOU HAVE TO ACCEPT THAT BOSSES DON'T KNOW WHAT THEY ARE DOING.

RULE 83

Accept That Bosses Are as Scared as You Are at Times

Poor thingss; they too get frightened, paranoid, lost, feel unloved, confused, vulnerable, and alone. Your job is to take away your bosses' pain and their fears and make them relax.

You are a manager and have to manage not only downward but upward as well. When you deal with your bosses don't ever

- Threaten
- Usurp
- Intimidate
- Pressurize
- Menace
- Disrespect
- Question (apart from under Rule 82)
- Undermine
- Ridicule

Instead you have to support, back, encourage, comfort, console, cheer up, relieve the pressure on, be utterly dependable, take the strain, guard the fort, and eventually perhaps replace them—with yourself of course.

Some bosses are so stricken with panic they are incapable of making decisions. You will have to make decisions for them and reassure them that everything is fine—the doctor is in the house now, and they can go and lie down.

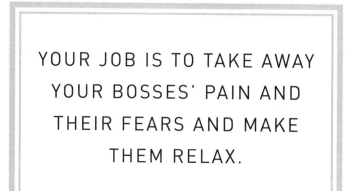

YOUR JOB IS TO TAKE AWAY
YOUR BOSSES' PAIN AND
THEIR FEARS AND MAKE
THEM RELAX.

RULE 84

Avoid Straitjacket Thinking

When you've got your head down and things are flying at you from all directions, it is easy to forget that you are supposed to be an innovative and a creative, cutting-edge sort of manager. We all do it. We get so close to the work under our noses we lose sight of the fact that we can invent, inspire, lead, motivate—and say "Yes." The team comes to you with a new idea and you are so weary from fighting the bureaucracy, the system, the weather, and the commuting that you just say, "No," no matter what it is they are suggesting. It's often a "No" with a subtext of "And leave me alone, I'm too busy/stressed/irritable to think about this now." Is that you? Bet it is sometimes. It's all of us.

So, we need to throw the straitjacket off. We need to lift our heads. We need to consider the options and think "Why not?" and "What would happen if we did this?" We need to stop being constrained by pressure and by work.

An easy way out of the straitjacket is to consider how you would view your job, your department, your team if you were a stranger coming in from the outside, coming in to do your job for the first time. What would you change? What would you leave alone? Think of what you're doing from the point of view of your customers—what makes sense? What doesn't?

RULE 84

It is easy to get so bogged down in minutiae that we fail to stand back and look at things with fresh eyes every day. But if we are to be simply the best sort of manager ever to roam the Earth, we must stay fresh or go the way of the dinosaurs. Staying fresh means being open to new ideas, new suggestions, new concepts, and new directions.

> IT IS EASY TO FORGET
> THAT YOU ARE SUPPOSED
> TO BE AN INNOVATIVE AND
> A CREATIVE,
> CUTTING-EDGE
> SORT OF MANAGER.

RULE 85

Act and Talk as if One of *Them*

OK, before you actually become one of them, you should be *practicing* to become one of them. If you are a junior manager, you should be studying the way middle managers walk and talk and be ready to become one. If you are a middle manager, you should be acting and talking as if you were already a senior manager. And on, right up to the top.

When I first became a managing director of a company, I almost forgot this Rule. I carried on managing as if I were a senior manager. But sales weren't going as well as I would have liked. I was organizing corporate sales and couldn't get to talk to the right people. I read somewhere that kings only talk to kings. I became a king. (Substitute "managing director" for "king" and you'll see what I mean.) Immediately doors which previously had been closed were opened and sales exceeded my expectations.

If you're going to be a king in the future, you had better start practicing now. Watch how anyone senior to you does things. The way they answer the phone, talk to staff, what they wear, what paper they read, how they get to work, what they do at work, and how they do it.

I recently met a managing director of a large company, and I was seriously impressed with how friendly and informal he was with his staff—who obviously adored him—and how genuinely relaxed he seemed. That is until we came to negotiate, when he was obviously totally up on his job and had facts and figures at his fingertips in a second. I watched him because he is my next step, if you like. He is my "one of them."

And no, no matter how high you go, you never walk on people—ever.

> IF YOU ARE A MIDDLE
> MANAGER, YOU SHOULD BE
> ACTING AND TALKING AS IF
> YOU WERE ALREADY A
> SENIOR MANAGER.

RULE 86

If in Doubt, Ask Questions

Why don't we ask questions more? Are we worried that people will think we don't know enough already? The smartest operators are those who do ask questions, all the time, and they invariably benefit from doing so. It's not so much a specific strategy for a particular purpose, as a general approach that can be helpful in all kinds of ways.

For a start you'll learn a lot more about your team if you ask them more questions: "Why do you think we're going about it in the wrong way?" "What do you think is slowing up the invoicing process?" "How would you tackle this customer?" And you may elicit solutions you wouldn't have done otherwise. And encourage them to express opinions or offer suggestions or submit ideas.

Asking questions is also a classic solution when you're in a tight corner. If you don't believe me, just listen to politicians being interviewed by pushy journalists. It's a standard response. When your boss asks you to explain something tricky, respond with, "Why do you think that?" or "Is this something our customers have been saying to you?" At the least it will buy you a little time, and at best it may provide you with usable information.

Questions are a great way to tell people they're being absurd without telling them they're being absurd. It's especially helpful therefore when dealing with inept bosses. Instead of saying, "That will never work" or something similarly inflammatory (if heartfelt), you just ask, "What outcome are you hoping for from this?" or "How do you think the design team will cope with that?" or "In what way will that improve our performance?" or "What effect do you expect that to have on sales?"

So long as you adopt a tone of friendly inquiry, it's hard to cause offense with a question. However it's an effective way to draw attention to the flaw in any plan, and to get other people to damn themselves without you having made any accusation at all.

It makes sense to ask questions about any new proposal of course, and generally people will. What's rarer is a manager who keeps on asking questions, even difficult ones, throughout a project to ensure that nothing is overlooked. But that's the kind of manager you're going to be from now on. Far too many people get the proposal accepted or the project launched, and then sit back and let it run. If it hits problems, they deal with it. But if you keep asking questions, there's a far better chance you'll spot the problems before you hit them.

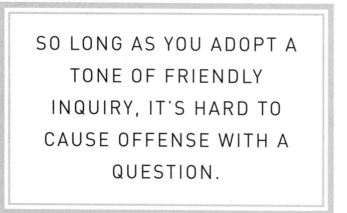

SO LONG AS YOU ADOPT A TONE OF FRIENDLY INQUIRY, IT'S HARD TO CAUSE OFFENSE WITH A QUESTION.

RULE 87

Show You Understand the Viewpoint of Underlings and Overlings

Being an underling—as we all know because we've all done it, been there—is tough. You get to take a lot of orders from a lot of people delivered in a way that puts your back up and makes you angry.

But hey, being a manager is often no better. Now you are caught in the middle. You get all that flak from the staff, plus all the crazy directives from the chief executive. You are no longer an underling and not quite an overling. You are the middle of the sandwich. You're going to get it from both directions, upward and downward.

One of the best ways to take the pressure off is to let underlings all know you understand their viewpoint. Don't just smile and say, "Yeah, I know where you're coming from," when it is plainly obvious you don't. You really have to make sure they know you do understand their needs and wants, grievances and demands, fears and hopes. Up and down the chain.

When push comes to shove, you are going to have to side with the overlings sometimes. When you think they are right of course. Your underlings—non-PC for team—will obviously resent this, particularly as they will not welcome any changes (especially ones they don't understand). This is a good time to let them tell you how they feel and tell them that you do understand this, and explain why the overlings have decided to do what they have.

RULE 87

If you're really good, one day you'll learn to explain how the underlings perceive things to the overlings, in terms they will understand—and vice versa. If you can get the underlings to see why the overlings believe that something not in their best interests makes sense, then you're on the road to becoming a managerial genius.

ONE OF THE BEST WAYS TO
TAKE THE PRESSURE OFF
IS TO LET UNDERLINGS
ALL KNOW YOU
UNDERSTAND THEIR
VIEWPOINT.

RULE 88

Add Value

Why bother to speak if you have nothing to add? And yet people do, all the time. They repeat what they said before. They rephrase earlier contributions. They say things that are completely meaningless. Why? How do they think this is helping? And why do they think they were asked to contribute if they have nothing useful to say?

Listen, if you want to be well respected, you should have listened to what was being said, read the information you were given, researched the background, thought about the issue—and formed an opinion that you can back up. On top of that, you should have come up with creative solutions, inventive suggestions, original approaches, and constructive ideas. Are you trying to impress people or aren't you?

You might find it instructive to listen to what other people say in meetings and secretly grade them on a scale of 1–10 according to how useful they are to the discussion. It will tell you a lot about your co-managers, and you should find that the high scorers among them are also the high flyers.

The people who have nothing to contribute but find something pointless to say anyway are not simply failing to help. They are actively wasting everyone's time. I've sat through meetings where if you cut out all the time-wasting ramblings from people with nothing better to say, you could slash hours off the duration of the meeting. This is not Rules behavior, and don't ever catch yourself doing it. You must be the one to set the standard—regardless of whether other people rise to it.

And you can be sure that while some of your colleagues may not seem to notice, your own managers will be well aware that you're someone to listen to because your contributions add value.

And what if you really have nothing helpful to say, or you've already contributed your thoughts and are asked again for your input? Well in that case, decline to comment. Politely say that you have nothing—or nothing further—to add.

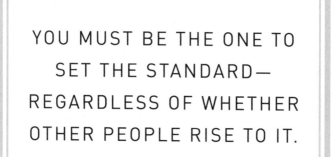

YOU MUST BE THE ONE TO SET THE STANDARD— REGARDLESS OF WHETHER OTHER PEOPLE RISE TO IT.

Don't Back Down—Be Prepared to Stand Your Ground

There will be times when you are certain and know you're right. In these times, sometimes you have to make a stand. You have to be prepared to put up or shut up. You have to be prepared to fight for what you believe in. If you are passionate about what you do, then standing up for what you know is right isn't that hard.

You don't have to be aggressive, just resolute. If you are being bullied, say so loud and clear—chances are the person harassing you will back off, quick.

You don't have to be rude, just assertive. If someone is spreading rumors about you or your team or your performance that aren't true, then confront them. State your position clearly, "I hear you are spreading such and such a rumor. This is not true and I would appreciate it if you would stop."

You don't have to be angry, just be very certain of yourself and very well prepared. If someone always finds fault with what you suggest, such as "Oh, that won't work; we tried it before and it failed," then stand your ground and don't back down. Say, "Yes, and here are the figures to show why it didn't work. And here is my report to explain why it will work this time and how it is different."

You don't have to get fired, just fired up. If you work for a boss who fails to give you suitable feedback, keep plugging away. Ask, "How can I improve my performance for next time? What steps should I take to get that pay rise I want that you've just said no to? Where do you see me in a year's time? What can we do to improve sales?" Keep pushing the ball back into their court until they are forced to give you suitable answers.

You don't have to be argumentative, just conciliatory. If you have a boss suggesting you cut legal corners, don't point-blank refuse and cause an argument. Instead say, "Ah. How would we handle this if the media/auditors got hold of it?" You aren't refusing but you are standing your ground and not going along with their ideas—and you are also offering them a way out. They won't have to make a point and impose their will on you, but they can now diplomatically back down without losing face.

> IF YOU ARE PASSIONATE
> ABOUT WHAT YOU DO,
> THEN STANDING UP FOR
> WHAT YOU KNOW IS RIGHT
> ISN'T THAT HARD.

RULE 90

Don't Play Politics

Politicians are people paid to play politics. You are not. You are a manager. You manage situations and projects. The people don't need managing. They manage themselves. Some of them go off the rails sometimes and play politics. You don't have to play with them. That's like playing on train tracks. You're bound to get hurt, bound to get run over by a train. Playing politics is using people to further your own ends, which, if you are playing politics properly, will be unpleasant, selfish, narrow-minded and petty. Playing politics invariably involves intimidating people, being sly, getting things done by lying or other dishonest means, not being yourself or true to others and generally behaving appallingly. There, I've said it now and I guess you know what I think of playing politics—it stinks.

You should "love thy neighbor, but pick thy neighborhood." Try to hang out with OK-people who don't feel the need to play politics.

Try to be involved with less popular projects because they attract less attention, less competition. Same goes for the less popular team or department. Here you can shine without having to compete all the time. Every company has people who get stuff done without back-stabbing. Hang out with these people.

Share information, always. This takes the wind out of the sails of those who do play politics. Be everyone's friend, so no one can accuse you of being cliquey or stand-offish.

Although you aren't going to play, you still have to be on your guard—be aware that playing politics goes on and be ready to deal with it in an appropriate way. Watch out for the hidden agendas that go on, the concealing true motives, the smear campaigns, the lying, the gossip (often malicious), the hints and subtle nuances that you aren't up to scratch or speed, the jockeying for power and control, the whispering, that sort of thing. If you are fortunate, you will encounter very little of it and any you do can be cut sharply off. Some industries seem to breed that sort of bad behavior and you will be hard pushed to stop it. Refuse to play, and get a reputation for being a straight-talking, unpolitical being—honest, above board, open, candid, guileless, and straightforward. Nothing complicated about you.

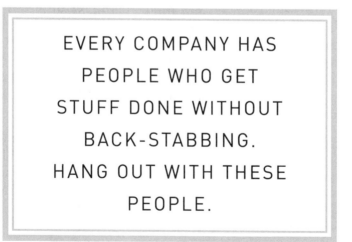

EVERY COMPANY HAS
PEOPLE WHO GET
STUFF DONE WITHOUT
BACK-STABBING.
HANG OUT WITH THESE
PEOPLE.

RULE 91

Don't Criticize Other Managers

Earlier we looked at how competition should spur you on and encourage you and how you should never be frightened of it. We were talking about the competition of other industries, other organizations.

But what of co-workers and other departments? Same goes. Don't be frightened of anyone or anything. If you are good at what you do, bold, creative, fast on your feet—as I am sure you are—then there is no need. If you refuse to engage in politics, then you will be seen as honest and trustworthy. You should never criticize, make inferences about, condemn, pass judgment on or whine about your co-workers or people from other departments/divisions.

If you do, you will be seen as weak or a poor performer. Sure, others will, and will be seen to profit from it at times. But do they sleep at night? Can they, hand on heart, swear they enjoy their job, or do they fear others calling them out as they have called out others? I think not. I've worked with quite a few. They harp on about how good they are, how bad everyone else is, but they quake in their boots privately because deep down they know they aren't as good at their jobs as those whom they criticize.

Just because someone points out your faults doesn't make you any less of an emperor, does it? And if you see another emperor with their new clothes, there is no point in pointing it out to them that they have been fooled—no one will thank you.

I worked with one manager who would jabber on incessantly about all the other managers and how bad they were. Interesting thing was every fault he pointed out, he was equally guilty of. We laughed because it was so obvious to everyone but him. He couldn't see he was highlighting his own faults.

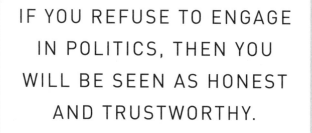

IF YOU REFUSE TO ENGAGE IN POLITICS, THEN YOU WILL BE SEEN AS HONEST AND TRUSTWORTHY.

RULE 92

Share What You Know

This Rule is about mentoring people who know less than you. They don't have to know that much less, and you don't have to know that much more. But if you share everything you do know, then they will know as much as you.

Some managers will see this as a threat. They are the foolish ones. What you have just done is train someone to take some of the workload from your shoulders. Someone to replace you when you get promoted.

Some managers feel awkward about sharing because they feel they don't know enough. But when you learned English at school, it was enough that your teacher knew about grammar and clauses and punctuation and that sort of stuff. You didn't need an award-winning novelist or a Nobel prize winner. No, just a humble English teacher was enough.

And what are you going to share with your team? That's easy. Anything that might help them do their job better: information, tactics, plans, skills, ideas, reading material, contacts, lunch—just keep giving them all the tools you can to make them more useful to you and to themselves.

Sharing with colleagues is important, too. The more you give out the more you'll get back. Suppose you give one bit of information to 20 other managers. If only half of them are generous enough to return the favor, it means you now have ten bits of new information to add to your collection. They have only gained by one but you have gained by ten—easy. They will invariably share with you, but not each other—don't ask me why. Perhaps they feel indebted to you and not to them.

SOME MANAGERS WILL
SEE THIS AS A THREAT.
THEY ARE THE FOOLISH
ONES.

RULE 93

Don't Intimidate

Being a manager gives you authority and power, no doubt about that. Perhaps that's what separates good managers like you from ineffective ones. You know how to handle that power and you don't abuse it.

People will look up to you as a manager, respect you, and even fear you. You have the power of unemployment or work over them, and they will be aware of that in all their dealings with you. But you have to try to overcome that by getting them to trust you. Always be predictable so that they know where they are with you at all times and you don't frighten them by catching them unaware. You mustn't abuse your position by intimidating your team.

Yes, there are two ways to get things done—fear and reward—and a lot of managers choose the first because they feel under-confident, unsure, and uncertain. Unlike you they aren't at ease with themselves, and this shows up in a threatening or bullying attitude toward their staff. We ought to pity them—or if we work under such a boss ourselves, try and get them better trained. Perhaps leave a copy of this book lying around for them to stumble upon accidentally?

RULE 93

A lot of managers don't know that their attitude sets the standard for how their staff treats each other and their customers. If they see a manager who is kind and cooperative, rewarding to work for and confident, it rubs off and they, in turn, act the same way toward each other and toward customers as well.

Working this way makes life easier and more productive. It's so much better to work in an organization where reward is used instead of fear to get things done.

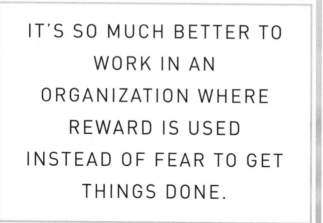

IT'S SO MUCH BETTER TO WORK IN AN ORGANIZATION WHERE REWARD IS USED INSTEAD OF FEAR TO GET THINGS DONE.

RULE 94

Be Above Interdepartmental Warfare

I once worked for two bosses at the same time. They were two directors of the company and they hated each other. Each had an agenda. Each fought a vicious campaign against the other with us managers—and staff—as their foot soldiers or pawns. It wasn't pleasant. They had their own areas of responsibility, and if you worked solely in any such area you were happy, because you had one boss. But if you, like me, had to cross over frequently from one director's area into the other's, then life was made intolerable.

The two directors countermanded each other's orders, played dirty tricks on each other, wouldn't speak to each other, and generally behaved like small children. I learned, and learned fast, to be a diplomat and a tactician. One director worked upstairs and one downstairs. I was sent up and down and learned to stop on the landing half way and stay there until each had forgotten what particular bit of interdepartmental warfare was going on. I also learned to play them off against each other to get what I wanted—but that was naughty.

I guess that was about as bad as it got, but I've also worked in companies where the rivalry between departments was extreme and interfered with productivity, kept staff on edge and contributed, I think, to high staff turnover. You would have thought the directors would have stopped it, but in my first example, you would see that even directors are capable of being silly and childish.

Don't you go the same way. Steer well clear of it all, if you want my advice. Be open and honest and upfront in all your dealings, and then you will get a good reputation, and no one will accuse you of being underhanded.

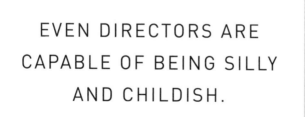

EVEN DIRECTORS ARE
CAPABLE OF BEING SILLY
AND CHILDISH.

Show That You'll Fight to the Death for Your Team

Your team is your tool for getting the job done—whatever it happens to be. Without your team—and that can be one lone person or thousands of people—you are nothing. Without your team you are an empty page waiting to be written—or typed. You must support your team, praise it, fight for it—to the death if need be. The brilliant manager—we don't need to say who that is by now, do we?—generates loyalty and respect by being the team cheerleader—that's you, that is.

You have to make people on your team see that you are not only their mentor, leader, guardian, and protector but also their champion, their hero, their defender. If anyone tries to criticize them, you will rise to their defense. If anyone tries to take advantage of them, you will rush to protect them.

On the other hand, you could always throw them to the wolves. See how far it gets you. But there are a lot of managers out there who seem to think that's the clever option, the right choice. What do you think? I've worked for and with some, and believe me they quickly lose staff.

RULE 95

If your staff has seen you defend them once, they will know they can trust you to have their best interests at heart. That if something unfair is being imposed on them, you will stand up for them. This also means that if you accept something, they are likely to accept it, too—which makes for a smoother life all around.

WITHOUT YOUR TEAM YOU
ARE AN EMPTY PAGE
WAITING TO BE WRITTEN.

Aim for Respect Rather Than Being Liked

Don't you just hate the manager who tries to be your chum, one of the guys/girls, your buddy, your pal. We've all worked with them and they are a mess. They embarrass themselves as much as their team. Aim for aloof. Aim for respect rather than being liked. Look, you want your staff to give you all they've got, not hugs and drinks down at the corner bar.

You have to create mystique, an air of power, authority, friendliness, without the desperate need to be liked. You have to remain detached.

Some day you may have to fire some of these people, and you don't need to make it tougher on yourself than you have to.

Some day you will have to promote some of these people, and you don't want to be seen to be having favorites.

They've got to look up to you, respect you, have you as a role model. They can't do that if you've been seen rolling around on the floor of the bar drunk as a skunk on a Friday evening, now can they? You can't create mystique if you try to be too chummy with them. Maintain a distance and they won't see it as stand-offishness but will respect the space you give them.

Maintain a physical aloofness as well: no back slapping, hugging, kissing, hair ruffling (hey, I had a manager who used to do this to me; I hated it and him—I was very young but that shouldn't have made any difference), arm wrestling (you could lose and you'd lose all respect then, believe me), office football, or any form of rough and tumble. Maintain your dignity at all times—and your style, credibility, sanity, and authority.

YOU HAVE TO CREATE
MYSTIQUE, AN AIR OF
POWER.

RULE 97

Do One or Two Things Well and Avoid the Rest

The really good manager is a specialist. You can't do everything. You can't do everyone's job. You can't do more than a few things each day anyway. Best to pick your specialist subject, be really, really good at it, and leave the rest to other people. In my company we have a very clear demarcation of who does what. I try to do as little as possible. I figure the better a manager, the less you do; it's all down to your powers of delegation.

So I stick to what I do best, which is basically talking to other managers. I don't do sales, but I do open doors for sales staff to walk through. I don't do key accounts, but I do set up contacts for our key people to follow through, and I do oversee the accounting staff. My "one or two things" is setting up meetings for my team to do the business, and overseeing the overall style of the company—its branding, its corporate identity, its place in the market. I manage the company but I don't do products.

I know my limitations. I know what I am good at and what I am bad at. I'm lousy on detail, routine, order, regular everyday stuff. I am good on sudden, unorthodox, interesting, one-off, people-orientated projects. I don't see what I am good at as being better, nor do I see the things I am bad at as being inferior. Quite the opposite in fact. I envy the ordered; those who can pay attention to detail, those who like to see a project through from beginning to end, those with empty in-trays and tidy desks.

What are you good at? And bad? How would you best describe the one or two things you could do well?

BEST TO PICK YOUR
SPECIALIST SUBJECT,
BE REALLY, REALLY GOOD
AT IT, AND LEAVE THE
REST TO OTHER PEOPLE.

RULE 98

Seek Feedback on Your Performance

Now usually we don't go round seeking approval because we can follow our gut instincts and we know when we have done a good job. But feedback is always a good thing. You should seek feedback from your peers, your rivals, your team, your bosses, and your customers. You are not seeking praise, approval or love, merely feedback. Remember you are all on the same team—from the janitor right up to the CEO, all kicking toward the same goal, all waving the same flag—or should be.

You should seek feedback to

- Identify your strengths and weaknesses.
- Compare the feedback with your own assessment of any situation—to make sure you are on track and realistic with your own self-appraisal.
- Learn from a situation where you went wrong—or got it right—for next time.
- Identify problem areas that need action and over which you have responsibility.
- See how your team is performing—as additional information to your own assessment.

See, none of this involves praise or approval (or love). It is a real-istic appraisal of a situation or project so you can learn and move on.

Now, how do you ask for feedback? Well, asking people on the team is easy, "So, team, how did we do?" They'll tell you all right.

Next, your boss, "So, Boss, how did I do?" Again easy.

Customers? Easy. "Is there anything we could do to improve the service/product/delivery times/specifications/proposal?" They'll tell you all right as well.

Co-workers? Just ask. "So, could you give me some feedback on how you thought the relocation went?" Or "Could you tell me how you think we (you and your team) did with the exhibition?" Or "Any chance of some feedback on the cost-cutting exercise/new accounting procedure/staffing levels over the summer vacations/new theme park ride?" Don't preface it with, "Can you tell me where I went wrong?" or, "I know the relocation went off appallingly but I don't know where we screwed up." Or even worse, "Help me out here, can you? I did wrong but no one will tell me what I did." Don't give anyone your judgment of the situation in advance. Let them tell you the good and the bad. Just nod at it all and say "Thank you" and move on.

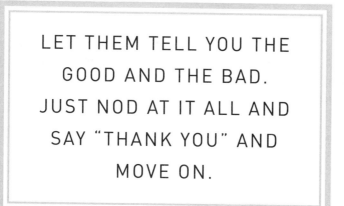

LET THEM TELL YOU THE GOOD AND THE BAD. JUST NOD AT IT ALL AND SAY "THANK YOU" AND MOVE ON.

Maintain Good Relationships and Friendships

I have a friend who has a catchphrase—don't we all?—and his is, "I don't see how that can possibly be good manners." He uses it if anyone talks across him at meetings or steals his ideas. I love it because it says everything about poor working relationships. Good manners—what a simple concept but how big a subject.

It is easy to maintain good relationships and friendships at work if you maintain good manners. This doesn't have to mean opening doors for people or carrying their briefcases. Good manners is being polite, warm, human, compassionate, helpful, welcoming—all the things you'd be for your customers, or should be. (I'm sure you are.)

This becomes tricky when it comes to somebody you don't like, have clashed with in the past, or who has been rude or unpleasant to you. But that's when it's most important to use this skill.

Even the rudest and most unpleasant person will find it very hard to keep being rude if you are pleasant, smiling, and open with them. (Especially if you can bear to throw in a little flattery about their expertise on a subject—if it's justified, of course.)

Try to see your colleagues as if they were as equally warm as yourself. If you always approach everyone with cheerful optimism, you'll find that they simply have no choice but to respond in kind. Offer help when you can. Speak to everyone as if they were your equal—as indeed they are. Look for the positive points in people—find something to like or respect about them and focus on that. Take as much time with the most modest of employees as you would with the highest. Treat everyone the same—with respect and decency.

IF YOU ALWAYS APPROACH
EVERYONE WITH
CHEERFUL OPTIMISM,
YOU'LL FIND THAT THEY
SIMPLY HAVE NO CHOICE
BUT TO RESPOND IN KIND.

Build Respect—Both Ways—
Between You and Your Customers

I was listening to a salesperson on the radio the other day, and the way he was talking about his customers made me think he and they were different species. He was condescending, patronizing, abusive, belittling, and ridiculing. He seemed to think it was fair to con people—he said it was up to us to check the small print, and if we didn't we were somehow stupid.

I have no respect for such people because of these attitudes—and the fact they phone me most evenings as I sit down to dinner with my children. I have a whole range of techniques to punish them for this, including pretending to be deaf and making them shout, saying they need to speak to my father, and leaving the phone off the hook until they get bored and hang up.

Don't cheat or lie to your customers. You need them. It's a two-way thing and it is an important relationship. Customers are never too much trouble. They provide my food and clothing and smart car and good vacations. Why should I abuse them? In return, I provide them with entertainment, fun, quality products, a brand they can be proud of, a lifestyle they can buy into, and a sense of belonging to an exciting and dynamic company. I respect them for what they give me, and they respect me for what I give them.

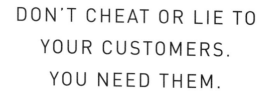

DON'T CHEAT OR LIE TO
YOUR CUSTOMERS.
YOU NEED THEM.

RULE 101

Go the Extra Mile for Your Customers

This is the easiest Rule of all. Going the extra mile should be the first thing on your mind when you wake in the morning and the last thing at night. Everything you do should be to take service that bit further.

Trouble is, customers are such a pain in the backside. They want stuff, they demand, they are difficult, they complain, they call at unnatural hours, they expect service above and beyond, they think the whole damn business should be run for them, they moan when we move our call center to India, they want money off, free gifts, two for one, buy one get one free, money back if they are dissatisfied, replacement products, guarantees, safety checks, harmless products. Gee, who do they think they are? Strike a chord here? Ring any bells? I've worked in industries where the customer wasn't so much king as an inconvenience.

Let's clear up one thing here and now. Without the customer there is no point. No point coming in. No point making anything. No point creating anything. No point doing anything. Without the customer we are all whistling in the dark.

OK, point made. Now we realize the importance of customers, we have to think of ways of getting them, keeping them, satisfying them, welcoming them, going the extra mile for them. We don't have to be patronizing but we do have to be creative in the ways we woo them. It's a lot cheaper to service an existing customer than to recruit a new one. Keep the ones you've got by being nice to them. Quick exercise: Think of three ways of going the extra mile for your customer right now.

WITHOUT THE CUSTOMER
WE ARE ALL WHISTLING IN
THE DARK.

RULE 102

Be Aware of Your Responsibilities

As a manager you have a responsibility to people on your team. You must make sure they don't come to harm while they are in your care. You have to make sure they are safe, healthy, cared for, well fed and watered, comfortable, kept well away from hazardous substances and equipment, and that they wear suitable safety clothing if necessary.

Now you also have a responsibility to the environment in much the same way. You mustn't do anything that is going to do harm, cause lasting damage, put anyone at risk of health or life, cause any land to be utilized in a worse way than it was before you came along. You don't have to be an eco-warrior, but you do have a responsibility not to cause harm or damage. Can you put your hand on your heart and say your managerial role is "clean"?

You have to have some principles—that you won't cause harm or damage. There has to be a line drawn—by you—somewhere, beyond which you will not go. You have to give something back. You have to be aware of what is going on around you. You have to be aware of what your industry contributes—or takes—from the environment.

This isn't stuff from the fairies or the hippies or the karmic religionists—this is real stuff. The more you put in, the more you get out. Be good and sleep nights. It's not a bad philosophy to live by and to manage with.

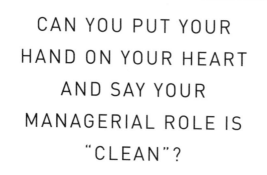

CAN YOU PUT YOUR
HAND ON YOUR HEART
AND SAY YOUR
MANAGERIAL ROLE IS
"CLEAN"?

RULE 103

Be Straight at All Times and Speak the Truth

This Rule follows right on from the previous Rule. Obviously if you think your boss is an idiot, you don't go and tell him—that's taking honesty just a shade too far. But don't lie, or cheat, or steal, or abuse, or defraud, or take advantage, or con, or trick, or swindle, or hinder, or worsen.

As a manager you have been given a privileged position—one of trust and honor. You are responsible for human lives—no, really, real human lives. You screw up and people get hurt. When they go home after working for you all day, they carry on living and breathing, feeling and loving, hurting and dreaming and hoping. You upset them or offend them or abuse them or lie to them and they take that home, and it affects their close family and friends and relatives. You must speak the truth to them at all times. If you can't say anything nice, say nothing, but don't lie.

Don't lie to your bosses. They don't employ you to do that. They employ you to be straight and to tell the truth. If you're not going to make your figures, don't fudge the issue—tell them. They can then take measures to help you or take action because your not making your figures might have a domino effect. They might be let down but they will be grateful for the warning. Better to know, than to hope and be disappointed.

Don't lie to customers. Obviously in all this there is a measure for artistic truth telling. If a customer asks if your products are superior to your competitors, you don't have to lie because they are—or you'd be working for the competition, wouldn't you? But if they ask if certain products have been successful and they haven't, you are entitled to creative truth telling. Say, "We have been somewhat surprised by sales so far but there is always room for improvement," rather than, "These really bombed but we're hoping you'll take a load off our hands."

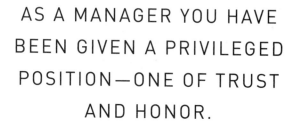

AS A MANAGER YOU HAVE BEEN GIVEN A PRIVILEGED POSITION—ONE OF TRUST AND HONOR.

RULE 104

Don't Cut Corners—You'll Get Discovered

Maybe you make airplanes—are you going to cut corners? Maybe use substandard metal in the wings? Replace the engines with junkyard replacements? I don't think so. You'd get discovered pretty quick. Hey, there is an increasing trend of taking managers to court if they have been responsible for injury to anyone using one of their products which has been found to be faulty (by way of design or manufacture or cost cutting). Quite right, too. If we were all made to be personally responsible for what we do in our working lives, maybe things would get a whole lot better. Rant over.

Maybe you don't make airplanes. Maybe you don't make anything. Maybe you just program computers. Nice and safe. Can't hurt anyone there can you? No? Sure? Think things through. Work out worst-case scenarios and be prepared for the fact that whatever we do as managers, we are responsible for someone or something that could get damaged, hurt, wounded, upset, impaired, killed—you name it.

Cutting corners ain't worth it—you'll always get discovered. I know you can get caught between the devil and the deep blue sea at times, with your boss telling you to do something and your principles telling you it is madness, but you need the job and the mortgage has to be paid, and it's easier to shut up and pretend it's all all right. But it ain't. You'll get discovered.

And you have to move heaven and earth to prove to your boss that cutting corners is a real waste of time. The old, "But what would the media/auditors make of this if they got hold of it?" argument often works wonders. As does asking about what insurance we carry or how the legal department has viewed this cost-cutting exercise. If you get told, "I haven't bothered running it past them," you can clap your hand to your head and shriek, "Oh, no, I'm working with a mad person." Using humor can get someone else to realize they have overstepped the mark and need to think.

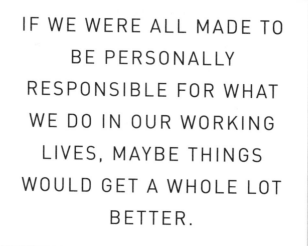

IF WE WERE ALL MADE TO BE PERSONALLY RESPONSIBLE FOR WHAT WE DO IN OUR WORKING LIVES, MAYBE THINGS WOULD GET A WHOLE LOT BETTER.

RULE 105

Find the Right Sounding Board

Management isn't easy. I mean, sometimes it all goes swimmingly, but sooner or later you come up against a tricky problem—handling someone difficult, finding the best way to address a particular challenge, deciding how to spread the budget around most effectively.

What you need is another pair of ears—a sounding board. It needs to be someone who understands the issues, so probably someone in the company. On the other hand, you shouldn't really be talking about these things with junior colleagues, especially if they involve other managers. But sometimes you don't really want to discuss it with your boss—definitely not a good idea if your boss is the subject matter.

It can be tricky to find the right person, but it's important that you consciously seek out someone you can talk to. Otherwise you will find some challenges much harder than necessary, and you'll also risk becoming so frustrated that you talk to the wrong people.

Your best bet is generally a manager as senior as you but in a different department. You need someone discreet who you can trust, and whose judgment you respect, and who will find time for you—it's no good if they're never there. And of course it's ideal if it can be reciprocal. You can both support each other, and that makes the trust thing much more balanced. No one's going to blab to your boss about what you said if they've also confided in you.

You don't have to limit yourself to one sounding board of course. It's not going to work if you discuss the more confidential aspects of your job with dozens of people. Even if they can all be discreet, which is unlikely—almost everyone will know your innermost worries and weaknesses, and you don't want that. However, you may find that you have a couple of peers who are useful sounding boards—maybe one who is very helpful with staff issues and another who has a really clear head for strategy. And sometimes someone outside the organization can give you a better perspective because they aren't bogged down in too much detail, in the way you are. Maybe your partner or a close friend or your mom or an ex-co-worker. Someone who will give you a new angle on things.

> YOU NEED SOMEONE
> DISCREET WHO YOU CAN
> TRUST, AND WHOSE
> JUDGMENT YOU RESPECT,
> AND WHO WILL FIND TIME
> FOR YOU.

RULE 106

Be in Command and Take Charge

You are a manager, so manage. Managing means just that, managing. Managing to work effectively. Managing to be in charge. Managing to be in command.

There seems to be a new movement in which managers are frightened to take command. They seem reluctant to assume control in case their team might resent this or accuse them of being a dic-tator. Nothing could be further from the truth. Teams with good, strong, commanding managers go a lot further because they know there is a captain at the helm. Without a captain we are all at sea—lost, scared, about to crash on the rocks. In a way it almost doesn't matter what captain we've got, just so long as we've got someone with their hand on the rudder. We all know the first mate does all the real sailing anyway, so the captain can be whatever, but the first mate can't function unless they know there is someone there, at the helm.

You've got to be a hero to your team and a good second-in-command to your boss. You have to be all these old-fashioned things:

- Dependable
- Reliable
- Strong
- Trustworthy
- Faithful
- Loyal
- Staunch

- Dedicated
- Accountable

And it's all a tall order, a tough call. But the rewards are immense. Being a manager is a fabulous job if you handle it right, abide by the rules and play it straight.

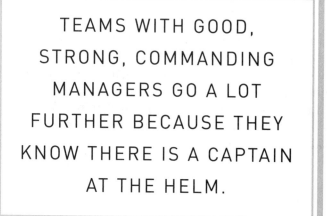

> TEAMS WITH GOOD, STRONG, COMMANDING MANAGERS GO A LOT FURTHER BECAUSE THEY KNOW THERE IS A CAPTAIN AT THE HELM.

Be a Diplomat for the Company

I hope you don't have to "kiss butts" to be a diplomat for your company, but diplomat you should be. The company you work for will drive you mad at times, and at others please you to no end. If you can stay away from the politics and backbiting that goes on in any organization, you'll be doing fine. Accept that every company has bad bits and good bits. Focus on the good bits and be incredibly proud that it had the good sense to employ one of the best managers in the business—you.

Speak highly of your company wherever you go and in whatever you do. This will get back to the head office and make you even more proud, because nothing generates pride better than being proud (the opposite of a vicious circle—a kindly circle?).

If you get a complaint, accept it, tell the person you will investigate, and get back to them—and do it.

Having to be a diplomat makes you question what your company represents—and that makes you question how happy you are working for them. If it is good and you are already proud—good for you. But if you have doubts, you might have to do some soul searching before continuing. Don't throw in the towel immediately—you might be of more use on the inside, changing from there.

Just as you would go that extra mile for a customer, find ways to go that extra mile for your company. This doesn't mean you have to be a yes-person or a lackey or a doormat. You can be strong, proud, independent, and rebellious and still be a diplomat for the company.

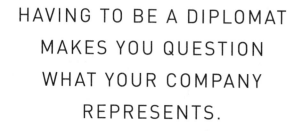

HAVING TO BE A DIPLOMAT
MAKES YOU QUESTION
WHAT YOUR COMPANY
REPRESENTS.

End Game

OK, no more Rules. This is your book. Keep it secret; keep it safe. If you don't let anyone else look at it, you'll be one step ahead without having to do anything else.

I have enjoyed being a manager immensely—am still enjoying it. It has brought me great satisfaction as well as considerable stress at times. But it has always been an adventure, always exciting.

Over the years I have discovered these fundamental Rules, which I don't think you'll ever get taught at a manager's training weekend or course. These Rules have sustained and kept me through many years, from a humble junior manager right up to CEO of my own company. I hope they will serve you as well.

I don't expect you to learn them all, do them all, agree with them all. But they serve as a useful stepping-off point for conscious decision making, conscious management. What they won't do is turn you into a goody-goody.

When I was researching this book, I talked to many other managers to see what secret Rules they lived by and was astounded to find a great many still lived by the "stab 'em in the back, claw your way to the top" school of thought. Sad really. They were all skinny and looked stressed, haunted, and unable to relax. The others, by contrast, who live by these Rules, seemed happier, more relaxed, and much more at ease with themselves and with their staff—and their staff respected them and enjoyed working for them and with them. Much better.

If you have any comments or indeed Rules of your own to pass on, you can email me at richard.templar@richard templar.co.uk.

Good luck with it all.

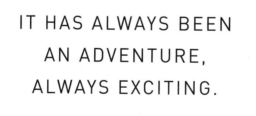

IT HAS ALWAYS BEEN
AN ADVENTURE,
ALWAYS EXCITING.